The Practice of Clinical Casework

Gertrude Sackheim, M.S., A.C.S.W.

Licensed Clinical Social Worker in Private Practice
Formerly Lecturer, UCLA Extension Division
Mental Health Consultant, Los Angeles County
Department of Mental Health

Behavioral Publications
New York

Library of Congress Catalog Number 73-19787
ISBN: 0-87705-141-0
Copyright © 1974 by Behavioral Publications

BEHAVIORAL PUBLICATIONS
72 Fifth Avenue
New York, New York 10011
Printed in the United States of America
56789 98765432

Library of Congress Cataloging in Publication Data

Sackheim, Gertrude.
    The practice of clinical casework.

    1. Psychotherapy. 2. Psychiatric social work. I. Title. [DNLM: 1. Social
service, Psychiatric. WM58 S121 p 1974]
RC480.5.S23   616.8'914   73-19787

Dedicated to the memory of

Professor Lydia Rapoport

Contents

Preface

It is customary for an author to acknowledge her indebtedness. Clients, teachers, supervisors, consultants, analysts, colleagues, friends and even a relative or two have all made important contributions. My debt to all and each of these is great. But separating the individual gifts of each is an impossible task. This book represents a synthesis of thirty years of experience, learning and cerebration. I have borrowed heavily from everyone. The following pages represent the convictions forged out of all these encounters. Responsibility for this end result must be mine alone.

Special gratitude must be expressed to Mrs. Katherine Handley, Dean Emeritus of the School of Social Work at the University of Hawaii; †to Dr. Kermit Wiltse, Associate Dean of the School of Social Work at the University of California at Berkeley; and to Mrs. Leona Schreiber, Director of Casework of the Family Service Agency of the Assistance League of Southern California. They so graciously provided the case material for Chapters Six, Eleven and Twelve, respectively.

†Deceased

5

Chapter One

Clinical Casework

Clinical casework is therapy. Good casework is sound crisis-intervention. As a profession, we seek a distinctive quality to what we do. We blind ourselves in our search for a distinctive descriptive label. Caseworkers do offer a service that is distinct and unique in many respects. But let us not, in the process of delineating our identity, do our profession a disservice by haggling over the word *therapy* and backing off in horror lest we be confused with other professions. We share with the other disciplines in the behavioral sciences a dedication to therapeutic intervention in the lives of human beings. The exchange and borrowing has been constant among all the disciplines involved. It is impossible to weigh properly the contribution each discipline has made to the others. Casework has made major contributions and has much of which to be proud.

It is this pride in the heritage of casework that is frequently overlooked and depreciated by the social work profession itself. Too often we confuse our programs with our techniques and claim credit for neither. Now that we are in the midst of a social revolution, there are pressures—both from within the profession and from the society within which we function—for changes and adaptations. This is good and healthy. But change does not imply that we have to start anew. There are basic casework techniques that remain constant and applicable in our new society, and caseworkers must hold on to them firmly.

There is a distinction between casework and social welfare. If this is kept clearly in mind, caseworkers will be less prone to sway in the winds of supposedly new fads and fancies, in the winds of so-called "new" clinical techniques. No technique is a panacea for all the ills of human beings and their society. Every technique advertised as new should be examined carefully: is it really new, or is it a new name disguising in somewhat fancier language a principle well-known and either already proven effective under a different name, or an abandoned technique which deserves to be revived and reenergized?

Any service is therapeutic that attempts to help individuals, families and groups to achieve a mode of living with themselves, and with others, that is more satisfying to the individuals concerned. The moment a caseworker asks a client, "How do you feel about this?" directly or indirectly, that caseworker is involved in a therapeutic process. It is precisely because many in our profession have hesitated to admit this, that there is so much confusion about what casework is and what it should be.

Because we are in conflict about our skills and services, our practice is often equally confused and frequently wasteful. Without a profound conviction about what we have to offer, we frequently find a lack of discipline and authority in our work. The word *authority* is not necessarily an obscenity. Here it connotes professional awareness of ourselves and our self-imposed limitations. We sadly lack the ability to say authoritatively, "This is what we do, and this we will not do." We must be able to spell this out specifically—first for ourselves. Then we will not need to explain ourselves so apologetically to others. Our public relations will improve as our self-image becomes more distinct.

If we examine closely the fashionable modalities in use today to try to help more troubled people more quickly, we can find the roots for many of these in sound casework practice, such as crisis intervention or family therapy. We have been remiss in our hesitancy to conceptualize what we do and to acknowledge its value until another discipline does so for us first.

The War on Poverty has posed many questions for all involved in the behavioral sciences, as well as for the providers and recipients of social services. Caseworkers who are rooted in their professional historical past will be less threatened and will be able to make a larger and sounder contribution to the formulation of "the Great Society." The old tried-and-true concepts form a foundation on which casework grew. Unfortunately, caseworkers have frequently tended to neglect these foundations, conceptually following the "new language" of "new" modalities. The basics often have been part and parcel of the new and fashionable. Like breathing, they have been often overlooked as an essential ingredient of function.

Casework grew out of material services to people. At first we were deliverers of food, rent, clothing, etc., ostensibly representing the compassion of the community. But no one can be interested in people for very long before realizing that people have feelings that influence their behavior. It is this acute awareness of the interaction between reality and emotion that has been and should continue to be social work's unique contribution to the broader field of therapy. Social casework must learn to regard itself with dignity as an equal partner in the group of professional disciplines that together form the behavioral sciences.

Casework owes a great debt indeed to the psychoanalysts. We have spent many hours acknowledging our debt. But we overlook the fact that caseworkers were eagerly searching for just such knowledge because they were aware of their need for a sound theoretical comprehension of emotional development and functioning if they were to continue to help people. Too often we forget that we have repaid that debt by supporting and defending psychoanalytic theory in the community. Most of all, we neglect the fact that we have made our contribution to the development of many psychoanalysts The psychoanalysts who have worked in and with social agencies are almost invariably those who show greater interest in families, reality situations, social pressures, etc. It has been a healthy and mutually beneficial cross-fertilization. It is also true that as caseworkers grow less awed by psychoanalytic teaching and practice, they are better able to use the psychoanalytic theory for the understanding of people and adapt this to their own basic philosophy and function. Casework may be psychoanalytically oriented, but it has its own milieu and technique. The discipline of agency limitation has forced caseworkers to be more self-disciplined in their treatment of clients. This sense of limitation and discipline is an invaluable asset, which this book hopes to emphasize and clarify.

There is one area which needs to be marked for special attention: that shadowy area called psychotherapy. Psychotherapy represents a broad spectrum of techniques for helping troubled people. Many different disciplines contribute to its varying techniques and function in various ways. It is the responsibility of the caseworkers in the field of social welfare to delineate their own contributions and limits. I submit that the psychiatrists who have had experience in working with social workers are usually better-disciplined therapists. They have learned a great deal from the hesitations of social workers. But social workers are so emotionally involved with psychoanalysts that frequently they know only that they have to be different and must not trespass on material that belongs only to the analyst and the couch. This is true. But where is the dividing line? How do we determine what we shall treat and what we shall not? How do we incorporate our base in reality with what we have learned about the unconcious?

Caseworkers must first extricate themselves from their transference and identification conflicts with their analysts. They have to take a long, hard look at what they do and what they can do. Then they need to be pleased with what they do and be proud to offer it as a method of choice in specific situations—not as a cheap, secondhand substitute for psychiatric treatment.

The caseworker also needs to clarify his position within the field of social welfare. Program planners, administrators, community organizers, activists for legislative changes—all are part of the broad field of social welfare. Casework is a specialty within that field. We live in an era of specialists. Rarely can one person combine several specialties successfully in his practice of any field. As standard bearers for the facing of reality by others, we must face our own reality. Sound casework demands highly trained skills, and caseworkers should not dissipate their energies trying to be multifaceted. Each specialty needs to have its own specialists with their own highly developed skills.

This book will attempt to present a practice of casework therapy that is structured and limited. It relies heavily on sound diagnostic thinking from intake to termination. It implies constant activity on the part of the worker. But this activity, like the traditional iceberg, is only visible in its smallest portion. It is the thesis of this book, that as the caseworker becomes more keenly aware of his therapeutic role, he will be able to help more people more quickly. More quickly may mean three years instead of four. It may be three sessions or three months. But that saving of time, even if only one year, can be vitally important to the client and the community. It is also the key to brief service when that is indicated.

When an individual comes to a clinic or agency with a problem, it is of utmost importance for the worker to be able to isolate the true problem that will be treated cooperatively by worker and client-patient. If this is determined at the beginning, the course of treatment can be defined. The possibility of being seduced into byways and blind alleys is considerably reduced. Each of us is the result of all our past experiences, intrapsychic as well as environmental. All of us could be treated for innumerable problems which would be apparent to a trained observer and only sometimes to ourselves. Caseworkers are not interested in treating the entire personality. They must treat that part of the personality which is causing the disturbance to the individual and those with whom he is in contact. The caseworker then has to evaluate what part of this person must be faced and whether the caseworker is the person to do it. The sooner this is isolated and related to the reality situation, the sooner will the individual be helped.

The casework treatment described in this book is based on the theoretical constructs of Dr. Sigmund Freud and of the analysts who added to his basic theories. It assumes familarity with these theories, since they are a regular part of the curricula of schools of social work. It is therefore assumed that the reader is at least in the process of achieving, or already has achieved, an understanding of the emotional development of "normal" human beings and is aware of the ways in which conflicts develop and are transferred into disturbing behavior patterns. This book therefore will focus on treatment rather than etiology.

Diagnostic casework therapy, therefore, is the treatment of that aspect of the individual that is causing him and his environment acute discomfort. An acute disturbance is one of comparatively recent origin which reflects a break in previously established, adequately functioning defenses.

The treatment of families is an important area for social workers. Emphasis on the family has always been an important part of the social work approach. It is hoped that the more secure the worker is with individuals, the sounder will be the worker's base in building techniques of treating families and groups.

While we will not concern ourselves specifically with the treatment of families as a group, we *are* very much concerned with the individual as a member of a family and the reverberation of his disturbance upon the homeostasis of the family. Therefore, any tool which is necessary for the welfare of the client will be utilized, (as indicated by the diagnosis. Even during social work's period of greatest preoccupation with intrapsychic processes within the individual, most practitioners continued to be concerned with the relationship of the individual to the other members of the family of which the individual was a part, as well as with his place in society. The diagnosis of a family is no different from the diagnosis of an individual. The same questions need to be asked and answered. What is causing the disturbance? Is it the intrapsychic conflict of the individual or the interaction between family members? Or is it the impact of the social milieu upon the family and the chain-reactive effects upon the relationship within the family? The sorting out of these factors will determine the course of treatment. Who shall be treated: the individual, the family or the community?

In this book are indicated only the broadest outlines of the casework structure within which the practitioner can function most effectively. The individual caseworker will take from this what he can use and integrate it into his own practice. No attempt is made to set down all the details of casework practice. This book is more an elaboration of a point of view than a detailed text for clinical casework practice. A logical premise could well be that the basic principle of a diagnostically oriented focus could be adapted to the special techniques and orientation of other fields of specialization within the field of social work.

Conclusion

Clinical casework is a method of treatment focused on the salient area of disturbance represented by the presenting symptomatology. It is a process of thought, not a categorization. The emphasis is more on the person in trouble as a particular person, or as a member of a family, not an abstract exercise in the exposition of psychodynamics. The hypothetical diagnosis at intake is not on the level of fixation or the usual diagnostic category, although these form the background in the caseworker's thinking and are essential tools in isolating the goal of the therapeutic process. The diagnosis is the isolation of the main conflict which is the underlying cause of the presenting symptoms. This represents the major change the client must make if he is to lead a satisfying, constructive life. This "kernel" of conflict must be phrased in simple, nontechnical language so that it is as comprehensible to the client as it is to the therapist.

Chapter Two

Intake

Almost as old as casework itself is the principle, "Accept the individual where he is and as he is." That is the beginning. The caseworker's identification with the therapeutic process of change confirms this. The caseworker respects what the client is as well as his ability and motivation to change. Acceptance of the individual's own levels of aspiration within realistic limits is an integral part of the intake process. The client comes to the caseworker because of some disturbance in his pattern of living. A social or personal disruption of previous equilibrium has precipitated a crisis.

Crisis and its precipitating factors were originally the warp and woof of the intake process. For a period, caseworkers frequently overlooked this. Now caseworkers often delegate this concept to the newly designated "crisis intervention" agencies, whatever their actual title. Yet this is the very area where social work had its special emphasis. Caseworkers who stay in the mainstream of their professional heritage are most skilled and comfortable with this emphasis in the intake process, and indeed throughout the entire therapeutic endeavor. The caseworker must never forget that the individual who comes for help has functioned in a personally satisfying manner up to this point. To paraphrase: "From equilibrium he came; to equilibrium the caseworker will help him return."

The format and extent of the unverbalized intake questionnaire in the mind of the caseworker should be predominantly determined by two factors: (1) What do the client's symptoms represent? (2) What is the function of the agency to which application is being made? Do these coincide? Is a referral elsewhere indicated? Obviously, a client in the "wrong" agency is not asked for the historical background of his symptoms. The focus of the interview shifts quickly to a clarification of the problem, a discussion of the "proper" agency and whether and how the client can get there. The needs of the applicant have to be correlated with the resources of the agency and the community. An important decision has to be made as to whether therapeutic intervention is necessary and available.

In this age of proliferating agencies the referral process requires close inspection. Caseworkers and the community in general are beginning to reexamine this shifting of human beings from one agency to another with no single agency truly assuming responsibility for a particular individual or family. In large urban centers a single family may have six to eight social agencies interested in the family at the same time, such as those concerned with public welfare, public health, schools, psychiatric clinic and/or hospital, probation, foster care, or vocational rehabilitation. Each member of the family has a problem that seemingly requires the services of a different agency. Each agency is aware of the familial interrelationships, but each says that integration of community resources is not the function of any particular agency. The multiproblem family can sometimes be the direct result of the multiagency community.

"One Family, One Caseworker" could well be a motto prominently displayed in the intake interviewing rooms of social agencies. When a family, or a member of a family, applies for a "new" kind of help to another agency, assessment of how this "new" problem fits into the pattern of agencies already involved with these people, is a most important facet of understanding the reality of the milieu that produced the problem and that will facilitate or hinder the resolution of the problem. The intake interviewer can sometimes become the integrator for the applicant. How much can be delegated to another agency? How helpful is it, realistically, to have sufficient flexibility in agency policy so that in certain instances, the staff members in several agencies become specialist consultants to the worker chosen as the significant helper to a particular family? The number of visitors and visits decreases, the numbers of human beings to which a single family has to relate decreases. Caseworkers talk a great deal about the importance of relationships in growth and development. Yet the same caseworkers feel intense frustration and subsequent hostility to families who have to relate to so many social workers of varying degrees of competence that they relate to none.

Integration of community resources is a valuable therapeutic function of intake interviewers in any agency. The time spent in this process is a contribution not only to the individual and family, but to the community as well. Despite the lengthy process of establishing interagency communication by telephone and by meetings, community money is saved by elimination of overlapping services and decreased hindrance to relationships and change. In addition, workers and agencies learn from each other how to delegate responsibility and how to establish and share common goals.

One woman on AFDC kept an appointment book so that there would not be excessive interferences with her housekeeping and management of her children and their clinic appointments. But she had no meaningful relationship with any one of them. The caseworker's therapeutic skills have to be augmented by the specialist's skills in such problems as vocational rehabilitation or adoption laws. But how much can be saved by one caseworker holding main responsibility for one human being or family? The diagnostic skills of the intake interviewer are important here. Is this individual only in need of services? Is the need for education in the use of available services? Or is this an emotional problem that presumes an ongoing therapeutic relationship where the services are incidental?

Mr. R. was a 32-year-old paraplegic who had had training and therapeutic help in the Veterans Administration Hospital following his release from the Army. He and his wife had made an excellent adjustment to this difficult situation. Both had demonstrated resourcefulness and courage. The adjustment, however, was predicated on their mutual interdependence. Mrs. R. was referred to a public health social worker because she needed to be hospitalized for tuberculosis. At this time the couple were receiving public assistance while Mr. R. was being trained by the Bureau of Vocational Rehabilitation. A child of Mrs. R. by a previous marriage was being seen at the school guidance center where both Mr. and Mrs. R. were involved in group counseling. What was the function of the public health caseworker?

First Mrs. R. was permitted to ventilate her fears and anger at this new catastrophe that had struck the family just as they had begun to feel that they were reestablishing themselves. From this outburst it became clear that the most important therapeutic relationship of this family was to the worker at vocational rehabilitation who had been seeing the couple regularly. It was he who had integrated the insights gathered at the school guidance center with the previous therapeutic history at the veterans' hospital. It was he who had helped Mr. and Mrs. R. through some of the difficulties of their public assistance application. A telephone call that took two days of persistence to transact finally made it possible for the vocational rehabilitation worker to arrange for a homemaker during Mrs. R.'s hospitalization. It was he who could become a major source of support to both Mr. and Mrs. R. so that the hospitalization became less disruptive to all concerned. It was he who became the liaison between the TB hospital staff and the family and public welfare and the school guidance clinic. But it was the alertness and prompting of the public health caseworker at intake that made this possible. This caseworker was aware of how to meet the dependency needs of Mr. and Mrs. R. quickly and effectively without increasing the dependency or attempting to explore it and interpret it. Their past history had demonstrated their ability to face difficulties with adequate support. By consolidating that support in the relationship of the one person, confusion and further delays were avoided. The time of the public health caseworker and the R.s' was not wasted in establishing a new relationship and, within the week, Mrs. R. entered the hospital as a cooperative patient, assured that her family would be cared for. Her trust and confidence in the vocational rehabilitation worker helped give her that assurance.

The therapeutic casework process begins with the first interview. It is the beginning of a joint task undertaken by two people who are mutually concerned about one of them. Its value and economy for both worker and client will be in direct proportion to the diagnostic alertness of the worker. The initial interviews place a heavy burden on the worker. He must begin to establish the broad outlines of the basic personality pattern of the client.

This is a threefold process: first, to ferret out the real symptoms and their precipitating causes (external factors); second, to limn the broad outlines of the defenses that have stood the test of time but could not withstand this particular pressure (internal factors); third, to begin to become aware of the defenses that can be subsumed under the heading of neuroses but will not be relevant to this therapeutic process. Sometimes these are left intact; sometimes some changes take place as a kind of chain reaction.

The intake process begins even before a word is exchanged. Both worker and client are observing and reacting, and the worker at least has begun to think, sift and question. Who makes the appointment? How does the client appear, wait, greet the worker? Who takes the initiative in beginning? What are the client's first statements? If more than one member of the family appears, which member presents the problem? What is the interaction between members? All of these are clues to the pattern of the client's personality and the disturbance that brings him for help. The course of treatment is begun with these first observations.

Then there are the questions to be answered by probing, listening and, as always, observing: what is troubling the applicant? What brought him to the caseworker at this particular time? The caseworker not only listens but pays close attention to the manner in which information is given. How does the expression of feeling relate to the material? Which areas seem most painful?

Where is the client most free? Where is he most restrained? What does he seem to be withholding? What
expectations does the client have of agency and worker?

Questions are directed towards clarifying the
symptoms and their genetic history. At intake, the emphasis is on establishing a mutual understanding that
the joint task of these two people is the acquisition of an
insightful attitude. Both worker and client then can understand from the beginning that as this clarification is
obtained, the goals of treatment are more clear. The ways
of achieving these also become more readily comprehensible to the applicant hitherto inexperienced in the therapeutic process. The intake interview is usually an initial and very different experience for the client. It is
sometimes difficult for the caseworker to remember that
what has become routine for worker and agency is
strange to the client—not only the physical setting and
the kinds of information required but also what the service will be. How is talking going to help? What will the
agency require? What does the agency plan to do? The
questions are innumerable but not abnormal.

The caseworker at intake and throughout treatment
functions on several different levels at once. He listens
and observes; he assesses the ego strengths and defenses,
evaluating which can be used, which need not be tam-
pered with, which need to be strengthened. He is constantly asking himself, "How does this particular statement or behavior fit into my understanding of this
individual? What is pertinent to question now, what to
accept and set aside either as irrelevant to the present
symptom or for later exploration? What is the problem
and its history? What do I know about the customary
genesis of this particular symptom? The client has told
me about the onset and course of his disturbance. How

does this confirm what I know theoretically? In what ways does this individual seem to differ from the theoretical stereotype?"

At some point, the worker indicates his interest in historical material as a basis for mutual understanding of the need for help. The present is, for all of us, the sum total of our past. As the client reviews his history, he may become aware of relationships between events and feelings. He may indicate them by association only. He may deny them completely. But he will almost certainly be aware that the worker sees a relationship between the two and between the past and the present.

As the caseworker is sorting out his first diagnostic hypotheses, his questions will be pertinent to these hypotheses rather than of the "tell me more" variety. The client's response may confirm, invalidate or change the original hypotheses. The worker's response will indicate quite clearly his understanding of the client as a unique person. The clarity of these responses sets the tone for further exploration and frequently stimulates freer expression from the client. The worker carefully phrases his questions to indicate the right of the client to reject its implication. This is an especially valuable tool for testing the client's strengths, insights and willingness to work on his problem, as well as an invaluable test of the worker's own flexibility.

A client may give information that is obviously impossible. This can rarely be challenged at intake. It assuredly is noted and added to the diagnostic armamentarium. And yet the uncritical acceptance can be mildly diluted with some evidence of the worker's honest reaction of surprise. Such statements as, "I had a *very* happy childhood . . . my parents were just perfect," may be met with a smile and tempered with a raised eyebrow, or an "Oh, is that so?" If the manner of the worker is neither hostile nor provocative, the client will later remember the worker's willingness to be both accepting and honest. The worker may well question to himself whether this was a household where emotion of any kind could never be expressed. Was anger too fearful for all members of the family? Is this relevant to the presenting symptomatology?

Once a relationship of mutuality of interest has been established, the client needs to understand the relationship of history-taking to treatment. The worker determines the need for direct explanation of this. Too often caseworkers take this process too much for granted. We forget that this is a new experience for the client, who often has no concept whatsoever of the therapeutic process. The client is entitled to a simple explanation of this and should be encouraged to ask questions, if he desires to do so.

The worker indicates that the request for history is a desire to understand the genesis of the client's problems. Providing the facts and feelings will point the way to a resolution and cannot be an end in itself. This will be indicated, again, by the worker's manner. At times it must be stated explicitly lest the client leave with the feeling, "I've told my story; now I have to return for the prescription: a blueprint of how to behave to change what is disturbing me."

The client may have legitimate curiosity about the worker's training. He may be frightened and using these questions as resistance. The questions, as long as they are pertinent, should be answered forthrightly. Thus at times resistance may be overcome without interpretation. With this evidence of respect from the caseworker as a background, the client can then be encouraged to talk about his feelings about asking for help.

Essentially the history is one of relationships: familial,

social, scholastic, occupational, the history of courtship, marriage, family planning, reactions to births, deaths, pregnancies, financial pressures or their lack. The list can be endless; the time is limited. Essentially, the worker selects out psychodynamically the "main theme" of the applicant's distress and how this has affected the various periods of adjustment. The client's deviations from this main theme are of important diagnostic value as potential sources of resistance or invalidation of the case worker's diagnosis. These are noted but not pursued. The caseworker is constantly assessing the ego strengths of the client. Which can be used? Which need strengthening?

The initial interview or interviews need not be an old-fashioned questionnaire. The worker's needs for information must not take precedence over the client's need to tell his problems and anxieties. But although the old-fashioned formal history was too restrictive, let us not throw the baby out with the bathwater. There are certain facts we must know before worker and client will know how to proceed together. At some point, the worker will have to interject this need to know these facts. Presented as part of the reality of the therapeutic process, this represents no threat to the client: "You've told me what is troubling you. Now let's try to understand how these troubles came about." If the history-taking remains disturbing to the client, this usually indicates an area that has to be explored before further treatment can progress.

The diagnostically oriented history-taking sounds like a lengthy process. The client who is voluble and takes a long time to ventilate urgent feelings will probably need more than one interview. The second should follow closely in time and be scheduled immediately. Even when faced with a torrent of feelings about a real pressure, the worker can find the occasion to indicate the worker's need to know more about the applicant in order to be helpful. In general, a well-focused interview, despite its necessarily tentative nature, can in the allotment of an hour or an hour and a half, make possible the determination of the client's suitability for and willingness to undertake the treatment offered by the caseworker. Depending on agency or clinic procedures, the worker may well be able to tell the client at the end of the first interview something about when treatment will start, who will be his therapist, and the possible frequency of interviews. Or instead, agency procedure must be made clear to the client so that the waiting period, if any, between intake and the regularly arranged treatment process, is comprehensible and tolerable to the client.

The client's feelings about coming for help are an important part of his process. Frequently, they are an integral part of the client's production of material about the precipitation of symptoms and the request for help. The omission of this is an important diagnostic clue. The worker's question may well indicate to the client that this is the first time that someone is interested in *his* feelings.

Mr. L., age 46, was referred to the clinic by a social worker who knew him personally. He had appealed to her for help because he was dissatisfied with himself and his lack of accomplishment and was constantly depressed. He functioned adequately at his job, was loved by his wife and two children, but considered himself a failure. It was the referring caseworker's impression that he was a perfectionist who drove himself too hard. He had made a number of attempts to seek psychotherapy, both group and individual, but treatment had consistently terminated unsuccessfully. The impression of the analyst who had seen him last was that this man was very bright and very capable, but was too well defended against his unconscious primitive anger to permit the use of deep insightful techniques. A supportive casework relationship seemed indicated.

We therefore started out knowing a great deal about this man. He had successfully frustrated previous therapists. He was still looking for help. He had chosen a female friend as his "last resort."

Mr. L. presented himself fifteen minutes early. He was familiar with clinical procedures and explained to the receptionist that he happened to finish his errands in the area earlier than he had anticipated. He was accustomed to being precise. His eagerness and conflict around dependency immediately became apparent. He was a tall, blond, thin man with almost an ascetic quality to his hollow cheeks and spare frame. In marked contrast were his full, quivering lips and the appealing, childlike look in his eyes. Here it is important to point out that physical descriptions are only meaningful when they add significant material to the worker's diagnostic understanding.

He began by saying that he did not know why he was coming except that he was desperate. All his life he had been a failure, but until the past few years he had had hope; now he was beginning to lose this. He had been born and brought up in a small midwestern town and had worked for many years as a clerk in a men's haberdashery. Gradually he had taken on more and more of the bookkeeping work. As the store grew, his activities became more limited to this area.

He seemed to meet the approval of his employer, became interested in accounting and enrolled in an accounting school. At the store, he had a position of increasing responsibility but always in relationship to a kind, approving employer. He came to this city on a vacation, met his wife on a prearranged date and was persuaded by relatives to marry her. Because it seemed like the "easiest thing to do," the young couple moved into the mother-in-law's apartment house, and Mr. L. found a job as an accountant through friends of his wife's family. He seemed to maintain the same close relationship with his new employer but was constantly driving himself to perfect his methods and set up better bookkeeping systems. Five years ago, he had saved enough money—"due to his wife's good management," he added parenthetically—to set up his own accounting business. He was painfully aware of his lack of a C.P.A. but managed to support his family minimally. He was constantly checking and rechecking his work despite the satisfaction and the growing number of his clients. He became increasingly dissatisfied with himself and his work; his wife no longer knew how to comfort him; his contacts with friends were diminishing—and so he turned to psychiatry. Here he is, doubting that anyone can help him. At this, he looked pleadingly at the worker, who replied by indicating that it seemed that he could be helped, but it was too early to know. The worker gave him the assurance of her confidence without giving him any promises.

The worker said he obviously knew something about the therapeutic process. He was probably tired of repeating his history, but sometimes a review brought up new awareness. He smiled and said he had learned nothing in his three years of therapy and could remember almost nothing of his early history. He was encouraged to tell what he did know, with the assurance that his lack of recollection was not unusual.

Before we begin the anamnesis, let us try to extrapolate what we know about Mr. L. thus far. First, we know he is depressed. Depression, we know, is anger turned against onself. What is he angry about—past and present? Are they the same? How do they differ? Perfectionism can be another source or result of anger. How come? What are his own expectations that all of his achievement is labeled lack of success? Why does he need to frustrate male therapists and then seek a female? Will he react differently to a female? Immediately, we begin to wonder about his parents. If he is so well defended against his unconscious, is there a danger of psychosis? Defenses that are well established usually are a warning signal: "Don't touch—except ever so lightly."

He presents himself early. He is anxious—always a good omen for treatment. Immediately, he tells the worker it is all up to her. His dependency seems more permissible with a woman. "All his life he has been a failure." In whose estimation? Why the discrepancy between reality and self-evaluation? His "success" was possible only under the aegis of an approving male employer who prodded and supported him in his progress. His marriage was arranged by relatives. The pattern of dependency becomes more and more consistent. The dependent man is a hostile man. The pressure to become an independent practitioner (to prove his masculinity?), to be a successful (?) member of society in the estimation of his wife and friends, had been successfully "comforting." Now her role was less effective. Why?

Thus we can see how much we learn and need to learn from a client's opening statements. We know this man is extremely dependent and is probably afraid of this. He seems to be asking for a relationship that will give him the assurance that his wife no longer promises. We can hypothesize that he also needs some ego support in recognition of his frustration at his inability to meet constantly increasing standards of performance. We can also make an educated guess that he needs help in reducing these standards to less than the gigantic size they assume for him. Based upon these hypotheses, the worker feels comfortable in offering the reassurance of her hopeful prognosis. This man seems to need the support of the relationship—not probing.

Now we are interested in the etiology of this symptom-formation. Immediately Mr. L. needs to challenge the worker. Previous therapists had not accepted him as he is. Would she? She obviously passed the test, because he immediately gave the following concise history.

He is the older of two children. His brother is ten years his junior. His father was a mechanic, a good worker but a poor manager. All of the business aspects were taken over by mother, who was so good that the business took more and more of her time, and the household was turned over to a succession of housekeepers. Mr. L. remembers his mother as a beautiful, energetic woman "who looked something like you." She was most concerned about the state of the patient's health and well-being. All Mr. L. can remember of his childhood was an unquestioning acceptance of his mother's unavailability except when he needed something, and an uninvolved acceptance by his peers in his community. He was an average student, an average ballplayer. He was part of his group but had no close friends.

The worker then constructed mentally a picture of an overprotective mother, competitive with father, whose role in the family was reduced to that of an accessory. Assumed also is the feeling of desertion and accompany-ing inadequacy which could not be verbalized by a small child overwhelmed by an "adoring," hostile mother. What could such a masculine child ever accomplish to please such a mother? The anger must have been felt as so overwhelming that only complete repression could guarantee survival.

A brother was born when Mr. L. was ten. There is no

recollection of the brother's birth or of any resultant change in the pattern of living. When Mr. L. was 18, he went to work after graduation from high school. Shortly thereafter his mother died. The business deteriorated. The Depression made work for father difficult. Mr. L. unquestioningly (?) assumed financial responsibility for the household, working longer hours to make his brother's continued education possible. His brother is now a successful lawyer, married, with three children of his own. He is energetic like mother used to be. The two brothers feel close but see one another infrequently and both are poor correspondents. The feelings of closeness come from Mr. L.'s recognition that the two can "depend" upon each other when necessary. The brother, however, is not aware of Mr. L.'s depression at present. They exchange communications about events but never discuss feelings.

Here we see more of the rationale for the anger and the dependence. Overwhelmed by mother's contempt for father, in which Mr. L. must have included himself, Mr. L. began the pattern of setting up impossibly high standards to win mother's approval and do better than father. Since these were never made explicit, they were always further and further away. The role of the father is questionable. One can assume some kind of positive relationship underneath his dismissal of the father as an ineffective member of the family. The positive reaction to kindly male employers would seem to indicate this. The confusion of male and female roles, his seeking for confirmation of his own masculinity as a "better" head of the household—all these seem to be subservient to the main theme of his need for feminine approval. The question of how and why his wife failed him still has not begun to be answered. His need to consider her "wonderful" and forbearing was so obvious that it was not questioned in this first interview. It is significant that he associated the social worker with his mother. He seemed to assign this role to the worker, who listened and accepted it. The line and goals of treatment already seemed indicated. The caseworker would assume the role of the mother with no hostility, more realistic standards and complete acceptance of the frustrations experienced in attempting to achieve unrealistic, undefined goals. The emphasis would indeed have to be on the "corrective" relationship. When and how to transfer this back to the wife would be an area for careful watching and weighing. The possibility of eventual joint interviews or corollary treatment for Mrs. L. would have to be constantly kept in mind. It is important to remember that it is homeostasis for the individual and his environment that is the primary goal of most casework treatment.

With these facts in mind, the caseworker informed Mr. L. that sessions once a week seemed indicated. This was a decision based on recognition of Mr. L's ambivalence about a relationship that might be too involved if too hurried. The worker recognized that Mr. L. might have many questions about this form of therapy, too. He could feel free to express this at all times. Progress is always necessarily slow. He would feel frustrated here, too. "Our job together" would be to recognize these frustrations as real to him and evaluate them objectively. Mr. L. smiled and said he understood. He was encouraged by the worker's faith in him. He didn't really feel he would be able to accomplish much, but he had to try. Nothing else was left for him.

It is towards the end of the intake process that the worker sums up for himself the answers to all the questions. Upon this he bases his first hypothesis. The worker not only reaches a tentative working hypothesis regarding the focus of treatment; he must also formulate for himself and his client the kind of treatment that then seems most appropriate. Is the conflict the result of intrapsychic disturbance or external pressures—such as socioeconomic—or would homeostasis be more quickly restored by focusing on the interaction between the client and one or more members of his family? It must be reasonably clear which members of the family are dynamically involved in this particular conflict. Would it be better to strengthen the individual in order to enable him to handle the interaction or would the intervention of the therapist provide a quicker and more economical means of communication between those concerned? Sometimes the worker will request an additional interview with one or more members of the family either individually or jointly. As always, this request must be based on the diagnostic evaluation of the factors precipitating the request for assistance. An honest explanation of this to the applicant makes him a more active participant in the therapeutic process. It makes clearer to him the meaning and goals of that process. It also should leave him free to reject the offer and to learn that the caseworker is interested in, and will accept, his feelings about this.

The applicant sometimes comes to a caseworker only because he is sent. He almost immediately announces his resistance and hostile obedience. The caseworker responds to his challenge with a nonhostile challenge. How does the applicant evaluate the referral? What is his understanding? Thus begins an educational process again based on a secure foundation of respect. It is surprising how often referral sources neglect to explain referrals in terms of the understanding and background of their clients. Lack of understanding is not necessarily a resistance. It can genuinely be based on lack of knowledge. Clarification of this at intake greatly facilitates the next step whether it be brief service, intensive therapy or another referral. Many applicants are lost when caseworkers ignore this need for education as part of intake. An unwed pregnant girl labors under the misapprehension that referral to a caseworker implies that she will be forced to give up her baby for adoption. A patient who consults a physician for headaches and is referred to the clinic caseworker feels the doctor thinks he is faking. A simple explanation of the interrelationship of emotional and physical symptoms brings relief. The more general the explanation, the more easily can the applicant accept it in principle, especially when the caseworker recognizes the right of the applicant to doubt the explanation. Citing an example of an obvious situation like panic in an accident calling upon the repressive forces to enable a person to function. Repressed feelings are like steam confined in a tightly covered kettle. They have to burst out somewhere, as in headaches. Always implied is the applicant's right to refuse to accept the explanation. But an exploration of the onset of symptoms and the circumstances surrounding the onset usually brings some clue the caseworker can question so that a whole new area of thought can be opened for the applicant.

Conclusion

The intake interview in diagnostic casework treatment is geared to a first hypothetical and tentative evaluation of what might be the major and primary conflict that is disturbing the individual requesting help. From the beginning, both worker and client become involved in a collaborative endeavor to learn what the basic problem really is, what caused it and what steps might be considered to restore homeostasis. Hopefully, this will illustrate the process of therapy. It is often possible and necessary to include some exploration of the client's feelings about coming for help, as well as the expectations of both worker and client. During the intake process the worker will begin to formulate the type of therapy which seems most suited to the problem thus "isolated," based on an understanding of the underlying dynamics of the situation as presented, such as individual, supportive, exploratory, group, family. The reality of what the community and agency have to offer is also an important factor influencing the decisions made at intake by worker and client.

Chapter Three

Treatment and Interpretation

Intake and early selection of the main street down which client and worker will travel together are so important that any discussion of methods of treatment is almost anticlimatic. As one patient observed, "No matter which curtain I pull up, the machinery behind it remains the same." This thesis cannot be repeated and emphasized often enough. The disciplined caseworker stays within the limits set for himself by his understanding of the client's presenting problems. The temptation to stray into other areas seen either by the caseworker or by the client as potential problems, must always be avoided. One of the greatest incidental values of a background of training in public assistance is that the very pressure of high caseloads forces the worker to concentrate on the most important needs of his clients. It is this kind of discipline that many social workers lose sight of in their headlong rush to integrate psychoanalytic theory and practice into their own practice, or conversely, into the pellmell anxiety to seem to "cure" too many people too quickly.

Mrs. D. had applied for help with the management of her sick husband. Her married daughter was involved in a difficult marital situation. Her second daughter was planning to leave college to work as a singer in a nightclub. Both of these situations were abhorrent to Mrs. D. who came from a wealthy, puritanical family. Although the initial request was verbalized in terms of Mrs. D.'s reactions to a diagnosis of terminal cancer, it was apparent that Mrs. D. was really asking for help in learning how to control all three members of her family.

Interview 1. Mr. D. has just had a series of tests. Mrs. D. thinks he should rest more. Mr. D. is rebellious. Caseworker questions Mr. D.'s right to respond to his non inner needs. Mrs. D. protests.

Interview 2. Mr. D. feeling better. Mrs. D. upset by quarrel between daughter M. and latter's husband. Mrs. D. thinks son-in-law is shiftless and irresponsible. M. has debased herself and her family by marrying him. They are living on a standard far lower than the D.s' have a right to expect for their daughter. Mrs. D. expressed this in a sympathetic manner, surprised that M. refused financial assistance. M. and her husband were receiving marital counseling. The caseworker raised the question with Mrs. D. regarding who set what standards. Mrs. D. left thoughtfully.

The next three sessions were devoted to Mrs. D.'s tearful, fearful reaction to Mr. D.'s illness. He had suffered a relapse and had been hospitalized. The caseworker's implied and explicit acceptance of Mrs. D.'s varied feelings about this, her fear of impending loss, her genuine concern about Mr. D.'s suffering, her respect for his response to his pain and possible death, and her appreciation of support she received from friends and family, as well as recognition of the special burdens the illness imposed on Mrs. D.

Interview 6. Mr. D. was better and home. This too represented reality problems of nursing and housekeeping. Mrs. D. permitted herself almost no time away from her husband. Her visits to the caseworker were her only moments of respite. Caseworker questioned whether Mrs. D. could not allow herself a little more real recreation. Mr. D. was encouraging her to do so. Caseworker helped Mrs. D. make more realistic plans.

Interview 7. The new routine had been established. Mr. D. could have visitors now but could not leave the home. Mrs. D. had returned to her bridge club and one of her philanthropic activities. Now she began to talk about Jane, the younger daughter. She revealed that Jane was really doing what she excelled in. Jane's success gave the family bad notoriety. Caseworker questioned whether it really was so bad. "Well," answered Mrs. D. "My friends are still my friends but . . ." and she went on at great length about her disapproval of Jane's career.

And so these three themes continued to weave in and out of the interviews for once-weekly sessions. The caseworker held to the theme of the right of these adults to self-determination and questioned Mrs. D.'s need to control them. Gradually it was learned that Mrs. D.'s father had been very seductive in his manner of constantly expecting her to take over for her own invalid mother. The seductive aspects of this were not explored. This, added to the growing realistic recognition of Mrs. D. that she received more love and respect from those close to her by being less controlling, set her well on the road to her own growth and development. She could say in her final interviews, "I still slip up now and then, but now I can talk it out and we all feel better."

In a more time-limited setting, Mrs. D. would have been "discharged" earlier with a label of success. Too often these labels highlight the first glow of intellectual learning and ignore the need for emotional integration of insight. Termination must be geared to the client's ability to function rather than to agency policy. The pressures of insufficient staff time to meet the expressed needs of people in trouble gives caseworkers added responsibility to sharpen their skills in order to help people more quickly. There are situations when caseworkers are forced by pressures to give inadequate assistance. But it behooves professionals to be honest about this and not proclaim necessary makeshift adaptation as an innovative psychotherapeutic procedure.

The "central core" might also be defined as that part of the problem which is the conscious manifestation of a deeper, more widespread unconscious "pathological" pattern. It is important to remember that the pathology often exists only in relationship to norms in textbooks. No one has ever found the ideal "normal" human being. The treatment of unconscious pathology is the province of other professionals—the psychoanalysts—when it is the major source of the pain felt by the applicant: the inveterate gambler, the angry, hostile person, the people with character problems whose acute distress is really chronic. These cannot be helped by caseworkers except in a very limited manner. They can be helped over a particular crisis with the recognition that recurrences can be predicted. Here very brief therapy is most effective. These can be subsumed under the heading of panic states. The very act of receiving true warmth and understanding from another human being cloaked with the authority of professional skill often brings great relief. This is an important contribution but should not be confused with therapeutic change.

Most people make various adaptations to their chronic pathology and live reasonably comfortably with them. When circumstances make this adaptation unworkable, the individual or family applies for or is sent for help. The caseworker then must distinguish between the basic psychological pattern and that part of the pattern which is in conscious conflict within the applicant and/or with the environment. The term "conscious" here includes the preconscious. This refers to those aspects of himself of which the individual is only dimly aware but which become clearer as treatment progresses. The caseworker treats only the "top layer" of the conflict. Frequently this produces some change in the unconscious as well. This is an incidental gain and is not the essential responsibility of the caseworker.

Mrs. Y. is a young, immature married woman of 24, with two small children. Her husband sent her to a family agency because she continued to have periodic mild depressions, neglect her housework and quarrel with him because she had never been able to pursue the career in which she had shown so much promise at college. Intake determined that she was an infantile-dependent character who chose her dependency as an expression of anger with a dominating father and husband. Although it was quite clear from the beginning that she also resented her feminine role, it was also obvious that this was an unconscious conflict outside the realm of casework treatment. Depression represents anger turned against oneself. This became the central theme.

One day she brought in a dream of being forced by her mother to go to a dentist to have her teeth removed. Her association was to the reading of a book on feminism which said all women should abjure housework, leave the children to others, go to college and pursue a career. She reported a long discussion with her husband in which she expressed her conscious opinion that a good home and emotional warmth in a home were as important as a career. Although it was recognized that this was a rationalization, she was actively supported in her position and emphasis shifted to her progress in disagreeing with her husband. She went on to elaborate how she was learning to be different from her mother, who always "submitted" to her father.

The worker clearly understands the client's underlying unconscious struggle regarding her femininity and acknowledges it in her support of Mrs. Y.'s conscious defense of her right to enjoy her role as a wife and mother. One can also speculate on the unconscious identification with the social worker. However, the interpretation was limited to Mrs. Y.'s right to her anger and the expression of that anger—the central core of her presenting problem. Again, the feminine role comes into question as Mrs. Y. begins to differentiate herself from her mother. An analyst might explore her identification with a hostile mother, envious of masculinity. The caseworker supports Mrs. Y.'s appreciation of her own "difference" as a human being with pride in the uniqueness that is the inalienable right of each individual.

The "central core" might also be defined as that part of the problem which is the conscious or preconscious structure which is a different manifestation of the unconscious conflict. The caseworker treats only the "top layer" of the conflict. Frequently this produces some change in the unconscious as well. But this is an incidental gain and is not the essential responsibility of the caseworker.

The nature of the presenting problem will to a large degree determine the choice of agency treating that problem. The nature of the agency will determine to a great extent how that problem is to be treated. In other words, the stated function of an agency will also determine which aspect of the disturbance will be treated. These lines may in time to come be somewhat blurred with the increase of generic agencies and generic caseworkers, but there will always be some lines of differentiation and therefore a different focus. The aims of a worker in a public assistance agency emphasizing rehabilitation will necessarily be somewhat different from those of a caseworker in a clinic or in a multipurpose family agency. An adoption agency differs from both. All may recognize the same problems, but each may choose a different focus. The goals of an agency and its administrative policy also determine the aims of both worker and client.

Helen came to an adoption agency for placement of her child born out of wedlock six months before. The father of the child had promised to marry her but had just left town with only a brief note to indicate he had no intention of keeping his promises or meeting his responsibilities. Helen had never wanted this child except as a weapon against Jim, the putative father. Now that he had gone, she was delighted "to get rid of the child, too." At intake, the legal aspects and involvements had been considered with Helen. She was 24 and had had many affairs before. This was her first pregnancy. She had left her parents' home at 18, presumably in rebellion against their middle-class standards. It was evident at intake that she had felt unequal in her competition with her beautiful sister and mother for her father's attention and had been acting out her hostility in her numerous affairs. Her child represented many things to her that she chose to deny. She had recently graduated from college and had immediately gone to live with Jim, who had supported her inadequately. She had never made an effort to support herself. Now she was frightened. Jim had left her very little money. She had insufficient training in her professional field, which required graduate degrees, and had no other training which would fit her for earning a living. Interviews focused on her plans for herself and her baby. Whatever ambivalence she had about the baby was thoroughly repressed and unconscious. Her rejection of the female infant was so clearcut and obvious to the worker and supervisor that it was decided to accept this without question. Interviews were therefore focused on the technicalities of adoption and Helen's plans for herself. The worker made available to Helen lists of scholarship funds, places of employment, counseling for part-time work, inexpensive residence recommendations. It was around this latter that the following interview took place.

Helen ruefully talked about her inability to live in a girls' dormitory. She was always getting into quarrels over trifles. She felt that she was "edgy" because of the need to live according to other people's rules. This was the first time that Helen came close to self-awareness. Heretofore, all her sessions with the caseworker had been a long series of complaints at all she had suffered at the hands of others, along with a realistic appraisal of her need to take responsibility for herself in the immediate future. The worker responded with approval for the insight displayed and used this to indicate how this self-awareness would help Helen plan more resourcefully. No attempt was made to explore the reasons for her rebellion against authority, her potential homosexual panic or other problems. Realistic plans continued to be made for her working, living and studying.

As Helen discussed her special needs for living and working she developed more and more self-awareness. This was in direct response to the new way of looking at herself and her problems, introduced by the caseworker's accepting yet questioning attitude. The structuring of the interviews by the caseworker emphasized the need to discuss all aspects of the reality pressures of employment, study and living arrangements. Evaluations of these pressures would determine which choices would be most suited to Helen. It was constantly indicated that each individual responds somewhat differently. Helen's unique needs were the concern of the caseworker and Helen. This kind of thinking, new to Helen, would help her make more realistic choices and give her greater assurance of being able to follow her plan to a successful conclusion. Implied, but not verbalized, was the need to inhibit impulsive acting-out. Also implied was the framework within which Helen, with the help of the caseworker, could begin to look at herself more closely. This in itself is a prideful achievement, aided and abetted by the caseworker's attitude of respect, encouragement, and approval or disapproval when indicated.

In one of the final interviews, during which Helen commented on the increasing number of restrictions she seemed to impose on herself, the worker introduced the possibility of therapy, describing the process and indicating the resources available. The last sessions were focused on a referral to a psychoanalytic clinic. Termination took place when Helen's plans for herself had taken concrete form: she had a job as a waitress with hours which permitted school attendance. She had failed to qualify for a scholarship and had to postpone part of her plans, but she had found a furnished room she could afford and planned to enroll in one or two courses as an extension student. She was also accepted as a patient at the clinic and was starting her therapy well-motivated.

The word *interpretation* frequently frightens or flatters the caseworker, depending on whether he is afraid to be confused with an analyst or whether he feels he can only be effective as a "junior analyst." Neither needs to be true. Any comment made verbally or nonverbally that helps another individual see his problem more clearly and thus eventually helps him cope with his own problems, is an interpretation. A raised eyebrow, a shrug of the shoulders, a simple "why?"—all these are interpretations representing as much profundity and real understanding of the client, and indeed at times even more so, than a long exposition of what the caseworker thinks about these problems.

The timing of interpretation is highly important and related to the worker's awareness of the client's level of insight. In the case of Helen, it was not until the accumulation of production regarding the difficulties imposed on reality by Helen's personality was conspicuously conscious to Helen that she was ready to accept a referral to a psychiatric clinic. The worker's alert response to the first demonstration of insight without overt interpretation of what the problem represented, laid the groundwork for Helen's reappraisal of herself based on respect for herself from both the caseworker and herself. Too often the beginning caseworker, especially, has such a need to demonstrate his knowledge—not only to the client but also for the record—so that the supervisor and consultant will also be aware of how knowledgeable he is—that the needs and readiness of the client are overlooked. A basic rule might well be not to make an interpretation until the client himself has made it so clear that the interpretation becomes a brief and succinct summing-up of what the client has already said. Thus Helen had already indicated in many ways her growing awareness of her personality problems and how they affected her reality. The intake worker might very well have come to the same conclusion after the first interview. But telling this to Helen would have had no effect, or at best a negative one at that time. When the constant evaluation of reality pointed up to Helen what her problems were, she felt supported rather than attacked and could accept a referral to a psychiatric clinic quite easily.

This does not mean that the caseworker cannot use interpretative questions early in therapy to start processes of thinking and open up new vistas for the client. But early "interpretations" must be tentative and phrased in such a manner as to leave room for comfortable denial by the client. For example, in the case of Helen, as she was complaining about all her previous roommates and her need to live alone, the worker might have inquired whether Helen had ever been aware of jealousy between herself and her roommates. This must be carefully phrased so that Helen can talk about how her roommates were jealous of her, or vice versa, or leave her free to reply simply, "No." The worker uses these questions as a kind of testing of insight. He must also be a very self-disciplined worker who is content with testing the insight and not need to push for more intensive exploration of the meaning of the jealousy, if admitted.

Interpretations should always be confined to a simple declarative sentence. If a lengthy explanation is made, it is usually indicative of the fact that the worker is unsure of what he is saying or of the timing of his interpretation. He is also subtly depreciating the client's ability to understand, and therefore is frequently saying the same thing over and over again with lots and lots of proof that what he is saying must be so.

The phrase, "a simple declarative sentence," is used illustratively only. It may be phrased as a question or an hypothesis. Rarely, except with adolescents and psychotics, is it stated authoritatively. It must be made clear to the client from the beginning that the therapeutic method of helping is a joint process. The client does the work. He talks about himself, his experience and his feelings. The caseworker's chief values to the client is the very fact that he does not experience what the client does and therefore often has a different point of view. This

latter point of view is of course influenced by his training. But at best the caseworker can only hypothetically
put the client's experience and the worker's knowledge
together to add up to an "it seems as though." It is the
client's right and essential task to validate or negate the
worker's hypothesis. If the client denies any interpretation, it is not valid at that time. A caseworker never can
truly convince a client he is wrong by argument. If convinced that the interpretation was correct, the worker
will wait for additional evidence and then repeat the interpretation. This process may be gone over many times
before the client is really ready to accept the interpretation and make it his own. A client once remarked, "You
used to make me so angry by constantly commenting
how fearful I must be of other people's anger and I've
always denied it. The other day, my little boy whose temper tantrums never disturbed me, suddenly started to
throw a ball towards me as part of a game, and in jest
said, 'I wish this were a bomb so it would kill you.' Suddenly, for the first time in my life, I knew what you
meant by anger. After the first moment of panic, I could
genuinely laugh with him. I knew at last what we had
been talking about for so long, and I was no longer
frightened." This paragraph tells us so much about the
young woman who uttered it. It would make a good basis for a "do-it-yourself" diagnostic exercise. Suffice it to
say that from then on, she became increasingly more
comfortable with her son. The presenting problem began to disappear quickly. Termination was not far dis-
tant. An analyst would have used this as a base for exploring the women's own basic and primitive hostile
feelings. The caseworker was content with helping this
woman be generally comfortable with the hostility she
met in reality. Her unconscious fantasies were permitted
to remain unconscious. Their surface presentation was
trimmed down and further repression encouraged. In ef-

fect, the caseworker taught her not to confuse fantasy with reality without exposing and exploring the fantasy.

The phrase, "a simple declarative sentence," also implies the use of everyday language. Professional terminology is jargon—useful jargon for the professional, it is true, but only for use within the profession and between the members of that profession. It is a kind of shorthand method of communication that has meaning only to those educated to the use of that particular language. Despite the sophistication of some of our clients, the use of our particular professional language is not helpful to any of our clients. The unsophisticated clients will not truly understand; the sophisticated client may think he understands and mislead both himself and the worker. Or there is the danger of the use of jargon as an intellectualized resistance which may please the ego of both worker and client but not truly add to the insight of, and be helpful to, the client. Nothing that cannot be said in simple, everyday language is worth being said. There is nothing that is implied in professional terminology that cannot be translated into everyday language. The use of terminology has too much the effect of widening the distance between client and worker. It emphasizes the authoritative, superior role a worker may, unconsciously, or consciously, wish to assume.

The use of the word *interpretation* frequently confuses the differences between supportive and insight therapy, especially for caseworkers overly eager to differentiate themselves from psychoanalysts. Most caseworkers have a psychoanalytic theoretical foundation in their understanding of people. It is natural to use some of their terminology. This becomes integrated into the professional lexicon. It has value in clarifying the caseworker's diagnostic evaluations and in communicating with other professionals.

All insight therapy is supportive. All supportive therapy is insightful. The depths of uncovering will vary widely, depending first on the client's presenting problem; secondly, on the client's level of integration as determined by the diagnostic evaluation of the caseworker; and thirdly, and only to a limited extent, on the skill of the worker. It has already been demonstrated that it is frequently far easier to tell a client something the worker is proud to know. It takes far more experience and self-discipline to withhold this knowledge and only tell the client what is pertinent to the client's level of integration and meaningful to him at any particular moment. It is true that the caseworker rarely deals with unconscious material. Most often, the caseworker is properly concerned with reality and the ego. But a new point of view, a new rearranging of facts, the elimination of distortion, frequently calls upon the preconscious knowledge of the client. It cannot be emphasized strongly enough that it is what the patient learns to know that is of greatest importance.

Free association is the province of the psychoanalyst because it is the road to the unconscious. This should not be confused with the voluntary production of the client which tells us something about his unconscious but more about the troubles he has been unable to communicate properly to anyone else before. "Properly" is used here to mean talking to someone who really understands. Understanding means being sensitive to the intrapsychic and emotional components of what is being said. This understanding is demonstrated by the caseworker's recognition of the implicit and explicit relevance of that part of the client's flow of language important to the client's development of growth and understanding in the area selected for essential therapeutic intervention. The freedom of the client to say what he feels is important to him, is essential for his own sense of self-respect and for the opportunity it gives the caseworker to validate or invalidate his hypotheses and to increase his knowledge about the client. This verbal productivity can be compared to a bucket of coal in which some gold nuggets are hidden. The client spills the bucket of coal. The caseworker finds the gold nuggets and holds them up for inspection. The client determines whether they are truly gold.

It is the function of the casework treatment to correct distortions. But the caseworker must be on guard not to feel responsible to correct and make reality more real just as a matter of principle. It is only when these distortions are pertinent to the problem isolated for treatment that they are valid material for correction, used here as a synonym for interpretation. Insight into the nature of such distortions adds to the cumulative effect of what is being learned. Insight into the nature of other distortions only confuses the issue and the treatment. Some defenses are best left well enough alone. Casework treatment aims only to modify those defenses that have not functioned properly and that have produced symptoms disturbing to the client.

Here again, the diagnostic skill of the caseworker is of paramount importance. When is it appropriate to patch up a defense? That is to say, when is supportive treatment indicated? When is it necessary to help a client give up a defense that is functioning inadequately and improperly and is wastefully exhausting the client's energies? That is to say, when is insightful casework treatment indicated?

Mrs. Ellen A. is 38 years old, married for 18 years to a man on the verge of a paranoid psychosis. She comes to the office referred by her husband's therapist. Her chief complaints (her term) and symptoms are uncontrollable outbursts of temper primarily directed at her three children, ages 16, 14 and 12 respectively. The history and her manner quickly reveal that Mrs. A. has always been confused about her own identity. She has always been extremely dependent, first on her mother and then on her husband, with concomitant hostility which frightened her. Unable to face her anger with the "essential" authorities in her life, she is freer to express this to her children. She realizes that the children are not the real cause of her anger, and for this reason accepts with alacrity the referral to a family agency. The caseworker probes gently but consistently for Mrs. A.'s anger with her husband. Holding firmly to the reality situation, the caseworker points out over and over again how Mr. A.'s unrealistic demands really infuriate Ellen. The worker's unexpressed permissiveness and acceptance of the hitherto repressed anger leaves Mrs. A. freer and freer to be more tolerant of her husband's illness. She begins to need to rebel less and less as she evaluates and respects her own needs and understands her right to refuse her husband's unrealistic demands. Equally, she learns that her children are individuals who are not attempting to "boss" her but who need her guidance, tolerance and understanding. For example, she had always resented working in the kitchen, making meals at all hours, cleaning up after the children when they used the kitchen. Being a wife and mother meant being a slave. Her mother had told her this would be her fate. It was hostile of mother to insist that Ellen marry Mr. A. Now she was condemned to give up her own interests in order to please her husband and children. In response to the worker's question as to why it had to be so, Mrs. A. responded with momentary silence. She then began swearing at her mother, ending up by laughing at herself for having been so blind. She very soon after rearranged her household duties so that she had more time to satisfy her own interests as well as to meet her responsibilities as a wife and mother. Meals were served on time. If Mrs. A. had time to clean up her kitchen, she would permit her children to use it and clean up as best they could afterwards. Little by little, she taught them what she wanted, allowing more generously for their mistakes. If she were tired and the children wanted to bake, she would explain quite gently that this time they could not do it. They had to respect her fatigue. In time she could even relax sufficiently to permit her kitchen to be somewhat messy.

So far, teatment has been largely supportive. Mr. A.'s illness provided many reality problems. Mrs. A. learned to be tolerant and then use the interview with the caseworker to blow off steam. Mr. A. would make demands, change his demands, be uncertain, ask for help from Mrs. A. and then scold her when she offered it. The worker's explanation of Mr. A.'s behavior (based on consultations with Mr. A.'s therapist) made Mrs. A.'s burden more tolerable. She was bright, and she wanted very much to preserve her marriage. She and Mr. A. had much in common and both felt the preservation of the marriage was very important. However, more and more interviews such as that described about Mrs. A.'s concept of herself as a kitchenmaid, indicated that the problem of female identification lay just under the surface of Mrs. A.'s weak ego. At a time when both Mr. and Mrs. A. were improving, the sexual difficulties between the two were coming to the fore. Since this was a family agency with a broad therapeutic policy, it was decided at staff conference that the caseworker, an experienced clinician, should continue work with Ellen.

The client indicated only a sporadic interest in sex. She blamed this entirely on her mother's attitudes which were taught to her: all men are beasts, and sex is something a woman has to submit to in order to keep her husband faithful. It was quite shocking for Mrs. A. to hear the caseworker remark quietly that women, too, had sexual desires and tensions. Ellen responded with a variety of fantasies about potential romantic lovers. The worker commented that she seemed to be afraid of the sex act itself. Following more material about Ellen's early concepts of sex as an attack, the worker was able to venture a connection between these concepts and Mrs. A.'s earlier material about her own hostility. Ellen was amazed to find herself talking about how much she hated men. They were authoritative, demanding and selfish. She herself could then make the connection between her earlier distortions about her need to submit to authority and the consequent need to "submit" to sex. Mr. A. was equally concerned about his fears of sexual and intimate relationships. Through frequent conferences between therapists it was possible to dovetail their therapy in tandem. Mrs. A. first, and later Mr. A., became less and less fearful of expressing affection for each other and then in turn less fearful of their own sexual impulses, which gradually became less hostile.

This latter period then could be considered more insightful therapy. It, of course, included a great deal of support. In the latter half of treatment, the worker was freer to interpret Mrs. A.'s behavior and attitudes. Her fantasies and feelings were explored on a somewhat deeper level than the realities of the first half. Yet the worker never deviated from the central theme: Mrs. A.'s fear of her own anger. In the first half, this was discussed only in terms of Mrs. A.'s feelings about herself. In the second half, more emphasis was placed on her hostility for others and her preconscious, somewhat repressed hostility to men. There were many times when Ellen could have been pressed into more details about her hostile fantasies and the gratification these gave her unconsciously. Instead she was permitted to use the sexual education she received from her mother as the major rationale for her behavior. Since this made her sufficiently aware of her own hostile feelings to ameliorate them, there was no need for further depth-exploration.

The concepts of resistence and ambivalence are corollaries to any therapeutic progress. Treatment is a learning process. No learning takes place without resistance. The meaning and timing of the appearance of resistance must be thought through by the caseworker. It may indicate a not-unnatural reluctance to accept an insight that is contrary to the conscious beliefs of the client. It might represent the client's fear of certain of his feelings. It may well indicate that the worker has made an incorrect diagnosis. And new, previously withheld material will emerge to indicate this.

Mrs. W. had been referred to a family agency by her physician because her anger about her arthritis seemed out of proportion to the disability. She herself was aware that her anger intensified her illness and was pleased with the referral. She was not aware of her anger with her husband. She had chosen him because overtly he was the precise antithesis of her father. Mr. W. had been an important student leader at the college they had both attended. He had been outstandingly successful in his business. It soon became clear to the caseworker that Mr. W.'s successes had been due to a combination of cleverness and his dependency on someone else: his roommate at college, his partner in business and Mrs. W. in his role as father and community leader. Mrs. W.'s growing incapacity was robbing her of her "secret" satisfaction in being the dominant figure in her household. The more responsibility Mrs. W. was forced to give up, the more inadequate she felt.

The central focus of the therapeutic intervention became an evaluation of how Mrs. W. could keep her role of control in her household without endangering the neurotic balance of the marriage. The first time the caseworker questioned Mrs. W.'s need to control her household, Mrs. W. reacted with denial. The incident began with the choice of a movie. Mrs. W. was angry because her husband replied that earlier in the day he had given one of their sons permission to see a movie. Mrs. W. disapproved. She felt the movie was too full of violence for an adolescent. A quarrel ensued. Mr. W. yielded. Mrs. W. remained furious. Why? Mrs. W. responded to the question with a long story about some lamb chops Mr. W. had brought home. These were not the kind Mrs. W. would have chosen. Then a neighbor telephoned and invited Mr. and Mrs. W. to a party for a charitable function Mrs. W. customarily supported. Mr. W. declined. Mrs. W. was planning to purchase some tickets anyway. The caseworker commented that Mrs. W. seemed to be displeased with her husband's behavior. Mrs. W. responded with denial. It was just that she had had no tolerance for any kind of frustration. She spent the rest of that interview talking about what a wonderful husband Mr. W. had always been. The caseworker, evaluating the shocked reaction of Mrs. W. which had been even more obvious from the intensity of her denial, decided correctly to focus in subsequent interviews on helping Mrs. W. reestablish her dominance on the household. Her physician agreed that she was not so sick that her children could not continue to come to her for advice and permission. Mrs. W. was encouraged to learn to shop by telephone. The telephone became a substitute for visiting friends. As Mrs. W. learned to accommodate herself to her illness, Mr. W. was relieved not to have to assume the "burden" of household responsibilities. Mrs. W.'s position was no longer threatened. She could then talk more freely about how frightened she really had been that she would become a useless cripple. Her anger had been an outlet for her fear.

Too often caseworkers have a tendency to regard material about daily living unrelated to the focus of treatment as resistance. The reality of the client is as important to him as his symptoms when both are disturbing. Or he may want to share an especially pleasing experience with the caseworker. The client cannot be as keenly aware of the segmented fraction of his experience which has therapeutic relevance. The caseworker has to respect this. If an event is particularly noteworthy, the actual therapeutic process may have to be postponed for half a session or even two or three sessions, depending on the genuine importance of the reason for the interruption, i.e., a death, loss of job, etc. The caseworker can almost always find a relevant clue to direct the client back to productive activity. It is not always necessary to point out that the client is resistant. Where it is obvious that the client is fearful, recognition of the fear is important.

Frequently caseworkers pressure clients into working through a resistance or overindulging the client's right to talk about anything the client chooses to relate. Neither of these extremes is valid. The worker must always question himself first as to the meaning of this resistance or intrusion and how interpretation will facilitate progress towards the predetermined goal. Then, by raising questions about this material, he can again confirm or negate his own hypothesis and decide how the client can best be helped.

Conclusion

Once the caseworker isolates the major pattern of behavior that is causing the disturbance to the client, the interviews that follow usually serve to confirm, but may negate, this conclusion. If negated, the worker must be alert to change his hypothesis and go on from there as indicated. In every interview, the caseworker is faced with the need to be selective in responding to and/or making interpretations related exclusively to the hopefully now-confirmed diagnostic hypothesis. It is wasteful and misleading for the caseworker to pick up the thread of every conflict thrown out helterskelter by the client.

Diagnostic casework treatment is oriented towards the goal predetermined by worker and client of a new level of functioning that will not only restore homeostasis but improve to a greater or lesser extent the previous level of functioning that had been satisfactory to the client. If the main theme is followed, treatment is shortened, and the client's self-awareness is deepened in a limited but effective manner. This does not necessarily mean that there may not be more than one central pattern of behavior to be worked through with any particular client. It does mean that it is wasteful and confusing to pursue too many insights at one time. The interpretations may be of past or present events. The caseworker may be illuminated by evidence in the transference, or in the client's interpersonal relationships. Resistance and ambivalence must be recognized and interpreted. All add up to a coordinated whole.

Chapter Four

Relationship and Transference

The term "transference" need not be another obscenity for caseworkers. Once again, we are dealing with nomenclature which, because it is borrowed from psychoanalysis, is frequently avoided out of fear, or overused and abused because of some workers' needs to be "as good as" the analysts are. The analysts often are the fountains of some of our wisdom. But because their brand of therapy is different, and, in a sense, more thorough, does not necessarily mean they are skillful caseworkers. For some analysts, the discipline imposed by the limitations of casework treatment requires a type of skill they do not develop. One of these special skills which requires a highly developed sense of discipline and special training is the use of the relationship with an awareness of the transference. In casework treatment, the transference is seldom used directly and overtly. Rarely is it verbalized for exploration or interpretation. But we cannot ignore the fact that it is present in every therapeutic relationship. In casework, we make every attempt to keep the intensity of the transference to a minimum. We dilute it by directing our interpretations away from the caseworker to other relationships. We attempt as much as possible to keep the interpretations of the manifestations of the transference on a reality level. We control the frequency of interviews with a view to keeping the transference as diluted as possible.

The relationship to the worker is a reality to the client. Except for the hardcore clients who have necessarily been subjected to a long succession of workers, the agency is secondary to the worker. The client may confuse the two at times. "Such and such is a good (or bad) agency because of my experience there," is a frequent comment of former clients. But the experience was with a caseworker. An agency's reputation in the community is only as good as its staff. Frequent transfer from one caseworker to another is like frequent transfer from one foster parent to another. A relationship that is meaningful becomes more and more impossible. The relationship of client and worker can become so overdiluted as to become meaningless.

A casework relationship is one between two individuals based on mutual respect. The client learns that he is expected to change to meet his own needs and goals. The caseworker offers him understanding, and respect based on that understanding. This element of respect and true understanding of the client's difficulties is an irreplaceable element in the treatment of human beings. It is this essential ingredient of "understanding" that is the core of the professional training and experience of the caseworker. This enables him to respect what others may criticize or reject. This enables the client to look at himself and eventually and gradually make necessary and obvious changes. Without this element of mutual trust and respect, no change can take place. The success or failure of any individual caseworker is in direct proportion to the integrity of his respect for people.

Social workers, like all other workers in the field of behavioral sciences, too often have a feeling that their knowledge about the emotional functioning of human beings gives them a superior status. Social workers, of course, do not believe this in principle, but their manner in social as well as professional situations unfortunately communicates this too often. Clients become a lower class. Anyone who is not a "professional" in the field of the behavioral sciences, and is therefore not in the know, is also relegated to this secondary status. The use of jargon to identify with this self-created "upper class" is an isolating device. A worker with this false sense of self-esteem cannot truly communicate respect to his clients. Caseworkers who approve of groups where everyone is laughingly exchanging comments about his clients who are unaware of their Oedipus complexes or their anger or whatnot, nonverbally tells his client that he, the client, is an object of scorn and contempt, no matter how he, the worker, may show verbal understanding of the client. It is true that sometimes these social exchanges are a way of letting off steam. But it is necessary for each individual to examine carefully his own reactions to each of his clients. The blowing-off of steam should be a conscious process shared with colleagues or supervisors in soundproof rooms in the office and not at social gatherings, restaurants or coffee shops. How many of us have had the experience of a client saying, "How can I trust you? I recently heard so-and-so talking about his clients. I surely don't want to subject myself to that." We may correctly interpret this as resistance. But reality is often a factor as well. Can we as individuals honestly assure the client that we, too, disapprove of such behavior? All the world loves to gossip, but let us gossip about our social friends, not about our client friends.

Confidentiality must be thorough and complete. We do not keep trust by merely not mentioning names. As a profession, we are always exceedingly cautious about disguising identifying information in reporting our work with individuals in journals or papers. We need to be equally cautious in our social manners.

An extreme example of this was the discussion about a client known to three caseworkers employed in a public assistance agency. The father in the family had been a well-known businessman who had been quite wealthy at one time. Without mentioning him by name, the three were talking in a bus about his uneasiness in applying for public assistance. A friend of the man, sitting nearby, overheard the conversation, recognized the man because of the unique situation and in shock telephoned the client to offer some help. The client, whose problems included depression, declined the help and told his wife how disgraced he felt. Thereupon, he left his home, ostensibly for a walk, threw himself off a bridge and was killed. Granted, this is an extreme and unusual example of how much damage can be done by indiscriminate gossip. Far more dangerous are the attitudes conveyed to nonprofessionals and past, present and future clients, that social workers really do not like people.

Since all of us have prejudices, the more aware we can be, the more pitfalls we can avoid. Some agencies could well reexamine their policies of assignment. A worker should have the freedom to reject honestly the assignment of a particular kind of client. This, of course, is possible only in agencies with smaller caseloads. The workers in agencies with large caseloads can be of greater help to their clients if they admit their prejudices to themselves. In any large caseload, there almost always has to be a choice of a few families who get more intensive attention. It would be unfortunate indeed if the worker could not include his own prejudices as one factor influencing his choice of clients for increased attention. This does not mean that the caseworker has the right to express his prejudice in hostile withholding or pressure. Only that those clients with whom he could not truly establish a respectful relationship would be relegated to the more routine procedures or in some instances, where possible, be transferred to another worker.

The entire concept of confidentiality is being reexamined. What is kept confidential, by whom and from whom, are factors to be determined not by rules and regulations and abstract principles. The reality of the individual's situation is now being included as a predominant factor in determining how confidential or "secret" material divulged shall be kept. It is a fundamental right of every client to expect that a promise made by the caseworker shall be kept. But should the caseworker promise to keep all the material confidential? We glibly say "yes" and think we do so honestly. But time after time, we break our promises, unthinkingly. A report to another agency may well be the first step in our unintentional hypocrisy. How often do we tell our clients about the existence of social service exchange, which are coming back into computerized fashion? How often do we promise to keep certain facts secret and then discover they never were very secret? This latter question becomes more pertinent when more than one member of a family is being seen by the same worker or in the same agency.

Mutual understanding and cooperation are essential ingredients of casework treatment. The goals are basically the increased ability of the individual to integrate the feelings and/or patterns of behavior that destroyed or disrupted his previous homeostatic behavior. During the course of treatment, there will necessarily be considerable acting-out of the disruptive behavior, unreasonable anger, or dependency. The worker's understanding acceptance of these deflects their force, in addition to affording opportunities for much-needed catharsis. Out of the respect of the worker for the right of the individual client to express his "differences" evolves a growing tolerance of the individual for those around him. In this way, families frequently benefit from the growth of one member of the family unit.

It is wholly within the function of the caseworker to use the relationship of mutual trust built up between himself and his client to assume the parental role, set limits to potentially destructive behavior. This need not be done in an arbitrary fashion. But no matter how it is done, the worker cannot ignore his authoritarian role: "If you do this, such and such will be the consequences." This still tells the client, nonverbally perhaps, that the worker really does not approve of such behavior. Depending again on the depth of the relationship, such behavior can be ameliorated and eventually halted because of the client's dependency and need to be a child. It may be the result of a process of identification with the standards of the worker. It may be the growing ability of the individual to assume greater responsibility for himself.

The first step in the development of a good working relationship is usually based on mutual respect and understanding. This is frequently a positive phase in which the client first has the experience of being understood and accepted. This is true even of clients who come with anger and resistance. The probationer referred by a judge may have to be very hostile at first and test his caseworker in many ways before the client can trust the caseworker. This may indeed be the essential first focus of treatment: learning by experience to trust another human being, especially one in an authoritarian role. But a working relationship has not been established until this is accomplished. Sometimes this is achieved in the first interview; sometimes it takes much longer. Part of the diagnostic process is the assessment of the readiness of the client to enter into such a relationship. During this period, the technique of exploratory interpretive questions is frequently a helpful tool.

Mrs. G., a 50-year-old married woman, sought help from a social worker in private practice because of her extreme outbursts of temper with her ten-year-old son. It was apparent at intake that she was unable to face her hostility to her husband, who symbolized her deceased father. Her son was the helpless victim of her anger with both. This woman, who had had a brilliant and successful professional career, still seemed to be a borderline schizoid character. Both her parents had been busy amassing a fortune. She had been reared by a succession of housekeepers. She had never been able to make friends of her own, depending on an older sister for social contacts. Reared in a small, close-knit community, her emotional isolation never was apparent. Her marriage had been arranged. It was in all its obvious manifestations successful. Mr. and Mrs. G. had many interests in common, and Mrs. G. protested much too loudly that she loved her husband very much.

It quickly became apparent that Mrs. G. had been looking for a mother substitute all her life. She had a vivid memory and had stored up all the experiences she had been unable to share with anyone, especially her husband, during all the years of her childhood, adolescence and marriage. For almost a year, she used her sessions to pour out these recollections. Some relaxation took place with this "emptying" process. Any attempt by the worker to focus on the reality was thrust aside as if Mrs. G. never heard what the worker was asking. Each interview began precisely where the last left off. It was only when Mrs. G. reached the present in her historical unburdening that she could tolerate the exploration of her feelings. At the end of therapy, she confessed that she was aware of the worker's attempts to focus on the present, but she was unable to acknowledge them until she was ready. She could not be ready and did not really trust the caseworker until she had fully "unburdened" herself. The caseworker's patience was the ultimate test. Secure that she would neither be rejected nor deserted, she could begin to explore the feelings of hostility which first brought her into treatment. This could well have been attacked as a manifestation of resistance, which in a sense it was. In this instance, it was recognized that the "resistance" served a number of purposes and was permitted to continue until the client was ready to move ahead. Mrs. G. had felt out of control all her life. Only this long recognition and acceptance of her right to be controlling left her free to work on her other problems.

Once a relationship of trust is established, the client is free to express his hostile, negative feelings. Although these are almost always transference manifestations, it is safer and more effective to direct the client's attention to the reality. Anger with the caseworker may be stimulated by some behavior of the caseworker: accidental lateness for an appointment, a cancellation due to illness or vacation. As such, it should be acknowledged. If out of proportion and relevant to the focus, it can smoothly be related to past patterns of behavior which produced the problem.

Mr. A. always lost his job because of his anger with superiors who did not keep their promises. He frequently ignored the reality reasons for this, feeling personally insulted and rejected, as he now reacted with the worker, who, in this instance, had not offered any provocation.

The anger might well be an overflow of hostility to a member of the family or a friend. Mr. B. complained that the worker was not interested, not helping, etc. Further discussions revealed that Mr. B. recently had a quarrel with his wife and felt guilty. He was afraid his wife would not really love him. Although it was obvious that he was testing the worker's interest by his complaints, the worker's silent acceptance of his complaints was sufficient reassurance. The caseworker focused on his fear of losing his wife's love, which was the conscious manifestation of his insecurity regarding his masculinity. He had originally come to the agency for help in securing complicated and expensive medical treatment. Although this treatment could be arranged with a minimum of effort on the part of the caseworker, Mr. B.'s mild depression caused by this precise insecurity had been manifest at intake. Continuing casework interviews had therefore been offered and accepted.

Unnecessarily cancelled interviews or those not kept without notifying the caseworker are also ways in which clients manifest their hostility to the caseworker. These can have many varied meanings, any one or all of which may be applicable. The client may be testing the worker's reaction, may be fearful; he may be demonstrating his need to control. The list of possibilities may be endless. It is the responsibility of the worker to relate this behavior to what is known of the client's personality problem and then to decide how this is pertinent to the focus. If it is not pertinent to the focus, a brief, relevant comment is sufficient. A testing dependent client can possibly best be served with a brief comment, such as "I missed you last week. What kept you?" Or, if the client says he was too angry, the caseworker may encourage him to talk about it rather than act it out—but should be careful to avoid making the client feel guilty.

The caseworker must be prepared to tolerate and accept without feeling personally threatened all forms of hostility in varying degrees. It is assumed by this, of course, that no patient is accepted for casework treatment, outside of a hospital, who is so psychotic that he will express his hostility in physical violence. Competition with a caseworker may be hostile but is frequently a step in the process of positive identification with what the client perceives as lacking in himself but in the possession of the caseworker. Rebellion against the caseworker may well be a testing of how much the client can trust the caseworker to respect his (the client's) uniqueness as an individual. Whatever the behavior of the client, whether during the interview or reported as having occurred outside the interview, the interpretation is always geared to the central focus of casework treatment. What can be learned about this person by both client and caseworker that will help the client integrate the new pattern of behavior essential to the reestablishment of homeostasis, as decided by both?

The interaction between transference and relationship can often be demonstrated in seemingly unimportant details. A depressed woman, Mrs. Ethel Y., who needed to act out some of her yearning for maternal solicitous care, became extremely dependent upon her caseworker. She was developing some intellectual and emotional insight into this. She was aware that often throughout her life she had felt strong desires to have her mother be alive again, only in a more giving and coddling role. In reaction to this, she often acted overly independent, giving to all, accepting nothing from anyone. Now, because of her depression caused by the sudden death of her husband, who had been more supportive than she had been able to admit, Mrs. Y. found her dependency needs completely unsatisfied and overwhelming. She constantly sought reassurance from her caseworker that she would get well. Interpretations centered around helping Mrs. Y. learn that she did not really need to be dependent or exaggeratedly independent in order to maintain her self-esteem. Mrs. Y. began to express her dependency needs, which had been so self-depreciating, and the depression began to lift. She constantly sought guidance from the caseworker regarding her plans for daily living. By returning the question and responsibility to Mrs. Y., the latter began to get more and more gratification from her ability to plan for herself and her family. One day the caseworker neglected to give Mrs. Y. the customary card with her appointments for the following month. Mrs. Y. left, saying nothing. That evening, she fell into a panic state and called friends to tell them she would probably need to be hospitalized. Her friends called the caseworker, who had already mailed the card with a note of apology. The caseworker was able to use this situation to deepen Mrs. Y.'s insight into her conflict between her dependency needs and her resentment of the power of the person she cast in the authoritative role. If the caseworker had not quickly realized the importance of her relationship to Mrs. Y., the depression might well have worsened, and the relationship might have become irreparably damaged.

A rather weird but true example of casework relationships and their effects involves Mrs. Sarah F., who had been receiving public assistance for many years during the Great Depression of the thirties. She was a childless widow without relatives, who applied for relief shortly after her husband's death. She accounted for the spending of the insurance left to her and then told a long and complicated story of having been cheated out of a sizable fortune by her husband's former partner. The first social worker checked on this in an interview with the partner, who produced ample evidence of the firm's bankruptcy prior to Mr. F.'s death. Mrs. F. was promptly labeled a mild paranoid and entry after entry recorded each successive worker's bemused tolerance of this "harmless encapsulated paranoid" who seemed to function adequately although she was somewhat withdrawn socially. This "bemused tolerance," it should be noted, always has a strong ingredient of contempt. No matter how this may be washed with friendliness, it is communicated. Several times psychiatric consultation was sought. It was always the decision of all concerned that Mrs. F. was harmless to herself and to others, and therefore it was not necessary to consider any commitment procedure. Psychiatric treatment was not considered advisable because Mrs. F. was obviously not accessible to therapy. She was firmly convinced that her view of reality was accurate. After several years of repetitious entries and routine visiting, the client was assigned to a student social worker in his second year at a local school of social work. The assignment was made to teach him something about psychopathology. This social worker, to his surprise, liked Mrs. F., listened carefully to her story and decided she was too lucid to be paranoid. The details of her husband's business had never varied from visit to visit. Mrs. F. appeared to him to be in command of her facts. He thereupon began to check more carefully. The training supervisor permitted this expenditure of time, expecting the experience to be instructive. To everyone's surprise, a thick file on Mr. F.'s partner was found in the District Attorney's office. Before long some of Mrs. F.'s money was recovered. What is most striking about this case was the effect on Mrs. F. of having someone believe in her after all these years. Although the money recovered was insufficient to do more than keep her off public assistance for a short period of time, she invested it in a small rooming house where she would have free rent and at least contribute partially to her own support. But even more important was the change in her attitude toward herself as a respected member of the community and her subsequent increased ability to go out, make friends and enjoy a more satisfying life.

The role of the caseworker is that of a representative of the community with a special coloration. He is the parent of either or both sexes; he is the teacher; he is the idealized version of all. In effect, he says to his clients, "The community has made it possible for me to be available to help you. During our time together, you and your problem will have my undivided attention. Whatever I say or do for you will be exclusively in the service of helping you alleviate the troubles that are disturbing you." By not reacting in kind to unrealistic expressions of hostility, tenderness, or whatever, the caseworker is focused on what in this materal is relevant to their job together. He therefore reemphasizes to his client, the salient aspect of the relationship, understanding, and its goal, the client's growth and development. This is usually the individual's first experience with a relationship devoted exclusively to his welfare.

It is precisely out of this aspect of the relationship that the danger of recklessness grows. Without the discipline imposed by the constant focus of treatment, both caseworker and client can easily be seduced into becoming aware of just one more problem and then one problem more. Before long the dependency is increased, the treatment is extended and the caseloads are overloaded. Then the community rebels and the caseworkers start overemphasizing brief, brief service. Without a philosophy of tightly disciplined focus of treatment, caseworkers often flounder about for arbitrary methods of dealing with waiting lists. Out of this turmoil, new and effective techniques are frequently evolved. By all means, let us keep trying new techniques, such as group intakes or family therapy. But let us not have to do so under pressure from unnecessarily long waiting lists.

As the client becomes aware of the helpfulness and

genuine interest of the caseworker, he will naturally want to use this service for more and more reasons: "I've done so well in learning about my relationship to my son, now I want to explore what is wrong in my friendships." Rarely is the request that specific or that overt, at first. Usually, it first appears in a reference, not necessarily casual, to a bad experience with a friend. This is frequently accompanied by a remark indicating an extension of the process of developing insight to an entirely new area. This is not an area that has been very troublesome or anxiety-provoking. It is here at the first indication of more avenues to explore that the caseworker has to guard against getting seduced by his own need to be helpful and his awareness that given sufficient time, he probably could be very helpful indeed. It is here that his relationship to his client is most important. The caseworker will listen with attention, but he is constantly searching for the first statement that will make a natural bridge back to the essential focus on treatment. For example, the friends did something that stimulated a reaction that is similar to the reaction that was causing the client's difficulties with his son. Or a question as to where the son was at the time may be pertinent. In any event, if the client has reason to believe that the caseworker is behaving in this way totally without hostility, and if the focus of treatment has been adequately established repetitiously before, this intrusion is perceived by the client as an extension of the interest of the worker and not a rejection. The client can quite easily follow the lead of the caseworker and return to the subject of focus.

Often the attitude of the caseworker is far more efficacious therapy than any verbal communication. It is this aspect of the transference translated into what Dr. Franz Alesander calls the "corrective emotional experience" that often makes for change and growth. Mr. Z.

came to public assistance with a long history of constant difficulty with coworkers because of his drive for perfectionism. He was an excellent worker who contributed services beyond the necessity of his particular area of responsibility. Although his employers appreciated this and regretted the need to discharge him, he was constantly a source of friction to other employees. He saw everyone's mistakes and let everyone know what they were. His own explanation was simply an inability to understand that other people were not as driven as he to seek perfection. The worker assigned to help Mr. Z. made little effort to interpret the lack of reality in such behavior. It was obvious from the history that this pattern was too well integrated and reinforced by numerous factors to make Mr. Z. available to any but longterm therapy, which was not available to him.

The worker instead chose to try to stimulate an ongoing process of trust and partial identification with himself. Over a period of more than a year, emphasis was placed on Mr. Z.'s real abilities and on the worker's lack of interest in what any co-worker might or might not be doing. The caseworker's attitude essentially was, "Does it really matter?"—accompanied by a shrug of the shoulder, a conspiratorial smile or whatever gesture came naturally at the moment. Mr. Z.'s father had been a humorless, rigid taskmaster. Mr. Z. had seen all of his employers as fitting into this pattern. His various discharges had been interpreted by him as proof of his inability to please anyone, no matter how hard he had worked. Gradually he began to regard "his" caseworker as a confidant. The material in his interviews centered around the stupidity of his coworkers and his bosses, who were unable to appreciate him properly. Assuming the role of the conspirator along with "his" caseworker, Mr. Z. was gradually able to limit his outbursts of criticism to his wife and caseworker and to try less hard to please his employers. "If those blankety-blank bosses were so blankety-blank stupid as to like only those employees who didn't care what happened, that's their headache." He found other ways of using his time in an obsessive fashion, but was able to hold a job for at least a year. This last period was determined by a followup study a year after the case was closed. At that time he was still working, living a rigid, isolated life, but one that was satisfying to himself and his wife.

Conclusion

Relationship is the more conscious aspect of the transference. Its use in casework treatment is limited exclusively to the implementation of the focus of treatment indicated for the individual client. The caseworker's role is essentially like that of an educating parent. His own lack of involvement in the problem permits the time spent with the client to be used in the exclusive service of that client, with the aim of restoration of presymptom homeostasis—a condition of personal balance between external and internal demands. At times the relationship is of paramount importance. It then takes precedence over the verbal communication. Then change may take place without insight, based primarily on a process of identification and/or interaction. Keen diagnostic thinking on the part of the caseworker is necessary to know when this is indicated. Even when the correlation of emotional distortion and intellectual recognition of reality is the goal, the client's reaction to the caseworker— and vice versa—is a contributing factor in the success of casework treatment.

Chapter Five

Dreams

Dreams are the royal road to the unconscious. Caseworkers are not primarily concerned with the unconscious. Both these statements are true. But, it does not
follow that caseworkers should not be concerned with
the dreams of their clients. Some caseworkers have been
"daring" enough to incorporate interpretations of
dreams into their therapeutic armamentarium. But rarely do they admit it in public or in print. What is so sacro-
sanct about dreams? Like any other life experience, they
admit of interpretation on varying levels. So may the
patterns an individual develops in the way he works and
plays.

Dream material is certainly not essential to casework
treatment. But it is equally certain that dreams can be
very helpful. They are most valuable as corroborative
evidence of the insight essential for the development of
the client. Since they are the client's own production,
they are closest to his level of emotional understanding.
Just because they are the essential tool of the analyst, it
would ill become caseworkers to overlook the value of

dreams for their own type of treatment. Caseworkers use them differently. The caseworker must be keenly aware of the limits of his treatment goals. Self-discipline is again most important. The caseworker may see much in a dream and the client's consequent associations but will only use those parts of the dream and the associations that are pertinent to the problem that has been isolated for the suitable treatment of the individual client.

It has been traditional to regard dreams as composed of three parts: (1) reality; (2) conflict, as demonstrated by its wish-fulfillment aspects; and (3) transference. All three of these may be used by the caseworker without delving deeply into the unconscious. The entire dream is not considered as material for free association detail by detail. Only those aspects of any one or all of the three factors that relate to the problem or problems under discussion are pertinent. The transference elements are not interpreted as such—this in order to avoid intensifying the transference neurosis. But as in all casework treatment, the derivatives of the transference as demonstrated in the reality living experience of the client are used, if relevant to the focus. The reality living experience includes the relationship to the caseworker. The wish-fulfillment aspect is usually most predominant if relevant to the material under discussion. The reality content is obvious.

There is a difference in the connotation of the term *association* as used by the caseworker. Free association is a process by which the analyst's patients let their minds wander freely in association specifically to dream material. The term *association* as used here refers to the more controlled spontaneous production of a client prior to or immediately following the telling of the dream. These are usually relevant to the dream content either as amplification or resistance, but the relevance may be obvious only to the caseworker. The interpretation of the relevant material depends on its relevance to the focus of treatment rather than on its relevance to the dream.

A client who has been struggling to overcome her identification with a rigid, self-righteous mother brings in a dream in which she has a quarrel with her mother and wins. She leaves the room triumphant. The caseworker smilingly congratulates her. Dreams represent our basic desires. It would seem that the client is more ready to free herself from the restrictive controls she had unwittingly assumed. It is significant that when the emphasis in treatment is limited, the content of remembered dreams frequently is also limited. It is as though the client is thoroughly aware of the narrow but specific goals of treatment, even on an unconscious level, and the unconscious reveals primarily that which will be useful to the dreamer. As long as the caseworker respects the repressions which necessarily must remain, the unconscious frequently helps keep them quite thoroughly repressed. This does not mean, however, that other material is never included in the dreams of social workers' clients. But more often than not, the other material is highly symbolized and inaccessible to the client without the tools of free association or interpretation. This inaccessibility must always be reinforced by the worker's silence. It is as though the worker and the client's unconscious are in league together to keep these other conflicts "secret," namely, repressed.

It is not always necessary to remind a client to remember his dreams and bring them to the casework interview. If they have relevance to the problem and are therefore meaningful to the client, he will not only remember them but bring them eagerly to the interview. Even if only preconsciously, he is aware that there is something in the dream that is going to be helpful. To ignore this by lack of interest is to be rejecting. We must always remember that treatment is a shared responsibility. The client who comes for treatment usually is even more involved in achieving certain goals than the caseworker. Since the major share of his energies is devoted to the pursuit of this goal, he is bound to use his night-time energies as well as those available to him during the day. It is, therefore, part of the caseworker's responsibility to accept this material too, and to help the client use this productively.

However, it should not be considered overstepping the boundary lines of social casework treatment for the caseworker to indicate that the client try to remember his dreams. It is usually wise to indicate to the client that dreams frequently are helpful but not always so. This gives the caseworker the opportunity to say, when necessary, that a particular dream does not seem to be relevant. Periods of resistance, confusion or doubt are all indications for a look at the client's dreams to see whether clarification can be found there. The caseworker must be careful to indicate to the client that the caseworker does not hold himself out to be an interpreter of dreams. But often the content of dreams throws additional light on the problem the two are working on together. The client is given assurance that dreams are not essential. They are, at times, just one more potential tool in the development of understanding oneself. It is well to point out that dreams of the night prior to the day of the interview are often more easily remembered. Dreams, like shorthand notes, frequently "turn cold"; an especially vivid dream remembered easily, however, can be just as valuable.

The client who comes for help for external reasons, such as unemployment, physical illness or adoption, is apt to remember fewer dreams than the client who comes for help because he is aware of an emotional disturbance caused by psychic tension. But even the dreams of the public assistance recipient whose only problem is unemployment are frequently relevant. A man who dreams he finds a suitable job is far more motivated than one who dreams he inherits a fortune and does not have to seek a job. Both are significant diagnostic indicators for the caseworker. Both can be used to the advantage of the client. The first man, congratulated on the depth of his interest in seeking work, finds increased self-respect in this acknowledgment from the caseworker. In the second instance, the caseworker is promptly put on notice that the dependency needs of this client are probably going to have to be faced before he can overcome some resistance to serious and successfully intentional jobhunting. A re-examination of the work history is clearly indicated.

Treatment is a learning process and follows the same path as all learning processes: two steps forward, one step backward and numerous plateaus. Proper use of dreams in the casework treatment process can frequently accelerate the learning process that is the growth of the client by development of emotional insight. It is helpful in pointing up resistance and in sharpening the focus of therapy for the client.

In the first stage of casework treatment, when the relationship is being established, the resistance is often to accepting the worker's interpretation of the problem. Harriett P., who comes for help with a son who is behaving badly, finds it very difficult to accept any responsibility for her son's behavior: "Just change Johnny, and we'll get along fine." She deflects all questions regarding her feelings about Johnny with protestations of love and affection. In the 24th session, she brings in a dream in which she murders Johnny by choking him. She awakened from the dream with great anxiety: Does this mean she really wants to murder her own son whom she loves so much? The worker answers directly: No, but it does seem to indicate that she has angry feelings about Johnny. Mrs. P. then bursts forth with a long story accompanied by many tears: Johnny was conceived before her marriage to Mr. P. Mrs. P. had had to give up a promising career to stay home and care for him. She had tried hard to be a good mother and conceal from everyone how much she resented being a mother. After this outburst, she and the caseworker were really free to engage in working together on the real source of the problem. The dream had been the crutch which enabled her, with the worker's help, to reveal her secret.

In the next stage of treatment, dreams are more important as reinforcements of interpretations. Here, too, they help the client to overcome his own resistances. A client referred to the social service department of a general hospital was suffering with ulcers. It was obvious to his internist that he was in great conflict about his dependency on his wife. He resented her tolerant understanding, correctly perceiving her unconscious, hostile contempt. His manifest pattern of behavior was total denial of all dependency needs. He was unsuccessful in earning a living and was totally unable to face his contribution to this pattern. His frequent change of occupation was always based on "reality." He was very bright and very capable of interpreting his reality in such a manner as to convince everyone, including himself, that fate was against him despite his efforts, his avowed sense of responsibility, and his real capabilities. He brought in much material indicating his denial of his wish to be dependent on the caseworker as well as on his wife, but consistently refused to see what he was doing. The caseworker accepted his complaints, made tentative efforts to point out his patterns, but made little headway. One day, about the

20th session, the patient brought in a dream in which he was a prince, sitting on a soft cushion with many attendants. His mother (now deceased in reality) hovered over him, bringing him various delicacies to tempt his appetite, often feeding him directly. The seductive behavior was ignored. The caseworker merely commented that his dream, too, seemed to indicate his great yearning for attention and affection. The patient for the first time poured forth an emotional outburst, weeping as he described how deprived he had felt as a child. His father had been crippled in an industrial accident; his mother had had to work to support the family from the time the patient had been an infant. The father, confined to a wheelchair, had proved to be an inadequate mother.

It is important to note in this connection that until this interview, this patient had been unable to recall very much of his early background. He had recounted the bare facts with seemingly no emotional involvement. From this time on, the patient worked far more easily toward acceptance of some of his dependency. As he clarified this for himself, his self-esteem increased. As he became confident of the worker's approval, he began to question his masculinity less. These became the side-effects and incidental benefits of his casework treatment, which was focused exclusively on his right to be somewhat dependent.

A similar use of dream material is the evidence it presents to the client of feelings previously denied. On occasion the caseworker, too, may be unaware that these feelings exist and how they are operating. Mrs. G. sought help voluntarily. She had had some psychotherapy previously but quickly discerned that her "therapist" was not truly qualified. She had a certain amount of sophistication about the treatment process and the difference in emphasis among the various disciplines. She related

easily and well to the caseworker and seemed adequately
involved in the treatment process. The purpose of seeking help was her relationship to her children now that
she was a widow and could no longer look to her deceased husband for support in rearing them. She felt lost
and uncertain. The focus of treatment was determined by
her consistent lack of self-esteem from childhood to the
present except when someone was present to reassure
her: first a brother, then a friend (female), then her husband. The caseworker was female. In the eighth interview, Mrs. G. brought in a dream in which her brother's
wife was involved in a scientific project that involved the
detailed examination of an insect. The incestuous wishes
for the brother, the jealousy of her sister-in-law, were
noted but ignored. For the first time since the intake interview when Mrs. G. indicated her eagerness for help,
the caseworker asked Mrs. G. how she felt about coming
for help. The response was immediate: Mrs. G. wept as
she said she was so grateful the worker had asked her
this. It was so difficult to understand why she hated coming to the office when she knew this was the place where
she needed to come. But she did feel like a bug under a
microscope. She was keenly aware of the worker's interest, but so much attention made her uncomfortable as
well. From there, she went on to her fear of being deserted. Her female friend had suddenly lost interest in
her, and she had felt awful. Now she was about to trust
another female and was terrified. She had lost her brother
to her sister-in-law and her husband in death. How
could she dare to trust anyone again? Her long, hostile
description of her girlfriend, and her sister-in-law in the
dream, seemed to indicate a longing for a masculine
caseworker. Only those who were masculine seemed to
be dependable. This, too, was not interpreted. The worker
turned the problem back to Mrs. G. with a question as to

why she could not depend on herself. The following sessions were concerned with the many realistic accomplishments of Mrs. G. As she compared what she had done with what she felt about herself, the lack of reality in her lack of self-esteem became clearer and clearer. She gradually assumed the proper authoritarian role with her children, to the relief of the entire family.

Contrary to psychoanalytic procedure, the caseworker need not wait for any associations in a particular hour before using dream material. If a client brings in a dream so symbolized that its relevant content is comprehensible to the worker and not to the client, the worker may offer an interpretation. The client's readiness to accept this and use it may well be a gauge of his progress. A client who is hostile to men brings in a dream of beating a horse and tearing off his tail in great anger because the horse would not obey. Following this, the client began to talk of how difficult it was for her to keep her appointments with the caseworker because of her work schedule. The caseworker knew from previous sessions that this client was resisting her hostile feelings about men, all of whom seemed overly authoritative and powerful to her.

Ignoring the sexual, castrating connotations of this dream, the caseworker commented only that a horse is frequently a masculine figure in dreams. The threat of uncovering her deep, murderous hostility was avoided. This brought great relief to the client. The client practically jumped out of her chair in her delight that at least in her dream she "could get even" with those horrible creatures. But she was rueful that in her dreams she was still powerless. The caseworker questioned whether the client truly was so powerless. The client then returned to how she hated men and all that she'd like to do to them. She was going to achieve a position of responsibility and then she'd show the men under her what a woman could be like. From here on, it was comparatively easy for the caseworker to point up the distortions in reality. Other similar dreams followed; all were used in the same manner.

Dreams often provide a missing link between the unconscious conflict apparent to the caseworker and its conscious derivative, which can best be dealt with by the social worker. A successful young secretary, Frances B., was constantly creating competitive situations with other young women. She had achieved her present position as secretary to the male vice-president of a large company by virtue of both her competence and her ability to demonstrate in many subtle ways her superiority to all the other secretaries. She drove herself to be indispensable to her boss, at the same time calling the attention of the next higher executive to her superior qualities as a secretary. The history indicated great hostility to Frances's mother, well repressed and compensated for. Frances was her mother's main source of support, did many nice things for her mother "to make up for father's indifference and contempt." Frances could recognize her yearning for her father in her need to please all of the male executives and her drive to go "higher and higher." She could not recognize her competition with her mother, and it was felt wisest to leave this defense untouched. One day she brought in two dreams, in both of which she was competing with her sister. Previously, she had described her relationship to her sister, three years her junior, as "normal." They had had the usual quarrels as children, but became good friends in adolescence and remained so. The dreams brought out most vividly Frances's jealousy of her sister. Hesitantly, Frances admitted that she had always regarded her sister as their father's favorite despite father's denials. The pattern of Frances's behavior and its rationale thus became much clearer, and Frances was well on her way toward resolving her competitive struggle with women. Her relationship to her mother did not interfere in her dating or other relationships. It was therefore permitted to remain undisturbed.

The illustrations can be endless. Dreams can serve any goal the caseworker and client together decide is pertinent to the problem and implement the achievement of their joint goal. They are an economical tool if properly used. Dreams can be a lever to propel into expression many feelings that might have been withheld, confirmation being provided by access to dream material. The caseworker is freer to acknowledge certain hitherto-withheld feelings and thus quickly dissipate fear and anxiety. In this manner, blocking and resistance may be overcome more easily.

Conclusion

Dreams are not an essential ingredient of casework treatment. When they are part of the reality of an individual client, they can be included as demonstrative of the process within the individual that is being studied by client and social worker together. They help reinforce interpretations, overcome resistances and point up material that the client might otherwise withhold. In every instance, only that part of the dream which relates to the constant central focus of treatment is utilized by the caseworker. As long as the caseworker respects the boundaries of casework treatment and the limits set by diagnostically focused treatment, he need not be fearful of including the interpretation of dreams among his skills.

Chapter Six

Cultural Factors

Cultural factors are often one aspect of the multitude of factors that make an important and pertinent contribution to the development of personality. As such, the caseworker must keep this possibility in mind and be alert to the cultural influence involved in the development of the symptoms presented by the client.

In its broadest sense, the constant ferment in and between various cultures is the history of civilizations and their development. The present conflicts, their erasure, resolution and emphasis belong to the field of social welfare with its proper focus on social planning. But broad cultural developments, with and without conflict, affect the individual, the family and the therapeutic group. In this sense, they must be acknowledged by the caseworker in his professional capacity as separate from his personal commitments as a citizen.

Each of us, at any moment in time, is the sum-total of all of our past experiences. Our first experiences are in the family, which is a subculture among subcultures amongst cultures. The earliest learning is in relationship to our parents, our siblings, our relatives. Only later does the child reach out to peers, neighbors, teachers, etc.—in other words, to society, friendly and hostile. At times, under certain conditions, the peer group becomes the more powerful carrier of culture with greater impact on the individual than the family. This is particularly true in adolescence. The impact is even greater when family ties are minimal. The peer group then takes over the role of the family and incorporates the individual into its culture. It is true that how the individual reacts to these experiences depends a great deal on his intrapsychic structure. The effect of an experience also depends on timing and coincidence. A child's fantasies cannot always be discerned by even the most astute and knowledgeable parent. For example, if the timing of a fantasy and a cultural prohibition coincide, the effect of the prohibition can be far more intense and traumatic than it might be otherwise. A younger child is more vulnerable than an older child.

So it is important in casework treatment, when considering cultural factors, to remember that these are just one facet of an individual's experience. The importance of these factors may be strong or minimal. The family, the society in which he lives, are significant, but they are not the only determining factors in shaping the individual. Equally, they are significant but not exclusive in shaping the deterioration of the previously maintained homeostasis. How and whether the cultural factors affect the symptoms, as determined by the request for help, is part of the diagnostic thinking and sorting out to be done by the caseworker. There are also times when withdrawal of cultural supports can be a precipitating factor in the production of symptoms.

Culture represents the homogeneous sharing of a

group of families. Human culture is impossible without the family to transmit it and support it. We build our culture on our sociability. We build our personalities on our learning within the family and society. The patterns of behavior that constitute the individual are adaptations to the family and society.

We know how the psychosexual development of the infant to child to adolescent to adult is based on the mores of the family. In our society, in the majority culture of the United States, the child is kept dependent for a long time, hopefully encouraged to develop a strong ego and learn the self-discipline of curbing his hostile aggressive drives. Under optimum circumstances, he matures into an adult secure in his sexuality and his ability to care for himself and to love and accept love. As he physically becomes an adult, he develops chronologically into a potential parent, in turn transmitting the cultural values he has accumulated and integrated. But, in our society, there are many minority cultures with different standards and different childrearing practices. It is important, therefore, to be alert for the differences that are normal for any particular individual.

Much has been written about the family as a biosocial unit in our culture and indeed in almost every culture that has been studied. The interaction between society, the family and the group has always been accorded scholarly recognition. It is only recently, however, that much attention has been focused on the family as a "treatable" group. Writers in the field emphasize the exploratory and experimental nature of their forays into this new area. Certainly there is much to be learned, but I think we are all a bit too timid. Caseworkers, especially, know a great deal about families as units. We, more than any of the other behavioral scientists, should be less fearful of applying all our so-called "new" knowledge to our "old" concepts of working with families. And we must always remember the effect of the family and the environment on the individual. All three interact in any culture. When the family fails to perform its necessary functions, we seek other social means to support it or restore it. We have to be careful not to replace it.

The current instability and rapid sociocultural changes have brought about the alteration of many social institutions and processes. We may well ask ourselves whether overemphasis on the individual has not helped produce more disturbance and less effective treatment in some instances. We have all felt helpless in the fact of impulse-ridden adolescents and have not been too successful in our attempts to reach their parents. Have we—the caseworkers, therapists, probation officers—intruded too violently into the family interaction to permit the normal processes of group control to function?

We have to be careful not to be led down a rosy path by some of the social scientists writing today. Most of them are thoughtful and are seeking earnestly for patterns. They find them. But each community and subcommunity is an amalgam of patterns. Ours is a highly complex society. And in our own observation of any particular family, we have to be very cautious lest we impose our preconceived ideas of a community on any particular family. How does this particular family see its own society? To what specifically is it reacting? Cultural traits are adaptive not only by another society but within a family.

In a predominantly white middle-class urban neighborhood, there existed a small cluster of "immigrants" from an Appalachian area. These produced an unusually high percentage of unwed pregnant girls. The social worker, new to this area, began by routinely asking whether the girls had considered placing their babies out for adoption. The response was inevitably shock and anger, and often termination of the relationship by the client. Subsequently, it was learned that this culture was completely matriarchal. Men were used as studs. It was customary for grandmothers to mother babies while mothers went out to work to support their families. Once this was clarified, the social worker and clients could work more comfortably together on what were the "real" problems as experienced by the client.

In severely socially and economically damaged families, realistic emergency measures are indicated as a first step. Our culture has built-in facilities for providing food, shelter and medical care in some areas. The skill of the social worker is equally great when he can recognize the need for these as the first and perhaps the only necessary action and takes steps to see that the community provides them. This is not always easy and frequently calls for imaginative creativity on the part of the caseworker. This involves diagnosis of both the community and the family. Sometimes this is all that is called for and represents an important contribution to the family as well as the individual. What is each ready to give? On what terms? A family of a minority group in an economically distressed area is not truly accessible to casework treatment if the community pressures continue to destroy what the therapist is trying to build. To restore social integrity is frequently no easy task; in some communities it is well-nigh impossible under present conditions. But even within such a destructive milieu, careful attention to family relationship is indicated. It is not true that we can only be effective if we focus on the family. In a milieu of destructive social patterns where the conflict is between cultures—such as American and immigrant—or between generations, and there is no dignity, no work or housing, only a strong family can survive. Some families can never be reconstituted. But the individual can be helped to face these realities and his strengths reinforced so that he learns to cope with them.

Whether a caseworker can battle all the social factors is questionable. But some help is better than none. Any person who asks for help is already willing to do battle with some part of himself or his environment. This in itself is an ally. The caseworker by his awareness of the reality of the sociocultural problems can be free at least to help the client ventilate his feelings about this. With this basis of honest recognition and respect, worker and client can then be less restrained in their joint task of treating those problems that are amenable to change. Equally, the ability of the caseworker to be aware of resistance based on an obvious social difference between worker and client, provides the client with the freedom to talk about his feelings, which if unexplored could disrupt the entire treatment process. Many of the dropouts in clinics and agencies can thus be avoided. The caseworker must include in his thoughtful diagnosis the question: how much of the behavior I am learning about this individual is culturally determined? What is intrapsychic? What is environmental?

Problems of social adjustment are not indigenous to particular social or economic groups. The economically depressed and the affluent are both often subject to extreme pressures. Much has been written about the social mobility of our society. This in itself represents a powerful pressure on the family which for any particular family may be destructive or constructive.

No one has yet discovered the final, magical answer to the widespread explosion of psychopathic behavior in adolescents of economically and socially deprived families, especially since in the process of their acculturation to the new mores there is so much expression of impulse acting-out. And what about the mores of the economically secure families who also encourage impulse indulgence?

The concentration of theoretical interest in the cultural aspects of the family was preceded in the history of our profession by a reaching out to anthropology. An attempt was made to integrate the studies of these behavioral scientists into our own. The social work profession has always been interested in integrating foreign cultures into our own. Its early beginnings in settlement houses had its bases in work with the foreign-born—the immigrants—and their children—the first-generation Americans caught in the crossfire of the pressures of the two cultures: their parents and their peers. Knowledge of both cultural patterns was essential to the worker attempting to help these individuals. But again social work left the research and theoretical formulations to another discipline.

It is impossible to learn all that is important in all the various cultures represented in this country and consequently represented in the caseloads of the various social agencies. It is possible and essential to be aware of the fact of cultural differences and the various ways in which they affect the individual. This kind of orientation sharpens the acuteness of the alert diagnostically oriented worker. How much of what a client says and does is influenced by his cultural background? The term *cultural background* includes not only his foreign heritage, if any, but such special influences as neighborhood or family.

For example, during the war a number of draftees who had a consistently, albeit modestly, successful history of accomplishment in school and job, developed transitory psychotic manifestations soon after induction. Often it was found that these men had been borderline psychotics reared in a small rural community where the population had been stable. Surrounded by friends with whom they grew up, taught in school by teachers who were familiar and nonpressuring, they graduated from elementary school and soon found jobs on the farms of former neigh bors who were in effect kindly and nondemanding parents. They often led quite isolated lives. They were not regarded as borderline psychotics in their own milieu. Thrust into a "foreign" atmosphere, among strangers, where isolation was almost impossible, they soon became psychotic. In rare instances it was possible to recreate, within the small Army unit, the familial tolerance and concern for this individual. These men recovered quickly. The culture of the Army was able to substitute for the culture of the hometown. Far more often, it was necessary to discharge these men, who then could return home and once more function effectively.

Conversely, a group of severely isolated alcoholics, having learned the value of group support, were encouraged to launch out into a community activity: a Christmas party for a small number of deprived children. They were able then to solicit community support, since they were not asking for something for themselves. The response was electrifying. They began to feel they could be respected members and did become functioning members of the community in which they lived.

In listening carefully to the historical material, the worker can isolate those facts in the client's development that were culturally determined. Their effect on the individual may be great or insignificant. The client himself may react as if they were not important. Yet the worker's awareness of these factors makes a difference in helping the client understand himself. Equally, showing understanding of certain social aspects of conflict makes the establishment of a relationship an easier, smoother process.

A family is a well-defined organization with its own history and dynamics that can be understood only in reference to the surrounding social system. The American family, culturally, is in conflict, with great emphasis on independence and physical separation, and at the same time equally great emphasis on togetherness and emotional ties. The economic structure has a tendency to keep the father out of the home at the same time that he is bombarded with propaganda about virile identification for and friendliness with his sons. The mother is equally bombarded with propaganda setting perfectionist standards for her performance as a housekeeper, mother and mistress, at the same time that personal achievement outside the home and family are held out to be more desirable. Frequently, the sole important function of the caseworker may be to act as the representative of society who lessens these pressures and brings them into a more realistic focus for the individual and his family.

We could talk a great deal about specific social pressures—ethnic groups, clashing cultures, or socially deprived versus power structure. At present, a segment of our society is greatly preoccupied with society's trend to a bureaucratic ethic, with conformity to an antiestablishment ethic threatening our morality of hard work, thrift and competitive struggle. Each generation presents its own conflict and its own built-in contradictions. It is important to remember that conflict is an integral part of the living process. It can be healthy; it can be sick. How the individual reacts to conflict with and within his culture are important diagnostic clues.

It is the function of the diagnostically oriented caseworker to search out the area of conflict that is incorrectly perceived and distorted and therefore cannot be compromised. When a conflict is culturally determined, what in another setting may be distortion, may well be a particular client's reality. An African college student in the United States may still believe in witchcraft and spirits. This does not make him paranoid. The difference in customs may make adjustments difficult until the differences are comprehensible to both casework and client.

What efforts—what defenses—has the client used to attempt to resolve this conflict? Substitution of one conflict for another, displacement from one relationship to another, increased rigidity or loosening of family ties— many modes are attempted. The greater the irrationality of the compromise, the greater is the impairment of the satisfactions in living in the society in which the individual finds himself.

It is important to be aware that there are many trends in our complex society. We may have and indeed should have our personal opinions as to which are pathogenic and which potentially constructive. But in our study of any particular individual in a particular culture, it is important to keep in mind constantly that people can only conform to the mores of a community on a flexible and selective basis. Generalizations are interesting and promote thoughtfulness. They rarely help the specific situation except to keep therapist and family within the same frame of reference. It is by a recognition of values that we attach meaning to differences amongst peoples.

Different social settings produce differences in value scales and social norms. The same action has a different meaning in a different frame of reference. These will influence the family's expectations of the therapist and vice versa. Caseworkers need to concentrate their attention on the subjective values of their clients. How they experience these differences is one key to our diagnosis.

We are now in the midst of a cultural revolution. Minorities are demanding recognition, respect and equal-ity. As in every revolution, there are excesses of violence and acting-out of various forms of rebellion. Here it is extremely important that the social worker examine his or her prejudices and adherence to stereotyped thinking. An individual dedicated to his culture may risk a jail sentence in order to prove a point. This is not to be confused with psychopathic acting out. A young man may appear with curlers in his hair as preparation for an "Afro" hair style in order to emphasize his identification with a segment of black culture. This does not imply that he is a homosexual. As long as the caseworker keeps the focus of therapy clearly in mind, he will be less likely to leap to conclusions and use them against his client. Cultural factors, like any other hypothesis, have to be tested against the client's conviction and his productions, verbal and nonverbal.

Much has been written about sociocultural factors. As Katherine Handley points out so well in her book, *Four Case Studies in Hawaii,** no community is so clearly a mingling of different cultures close to the source as is the State of Hawaii. The bearers of the "foreign culture" are still the parental figures. The somewhat more acculturated younger generations are still strongly affected by the culture of their origin in both positive and negative patterns. The rate of juvenile delinquency is high. This represents, as Mrs. Handley tells us, not only the conflict of youngsters caught between two cultures, but also the fact that what is "normal" to one culture—Hawaiian borrowing—is "delinquent" in another—American stealing. The caseworker must needs be an interpreter of both in such instances. This, of course, implies the caseworker's role in the community, which is another topic not within the purview of this book. But it is one to give

*Four Case Studies in Hawaii, Katherine Newkirk Handley, University of Hawaii Press, Honolulu, Hawaii 1961.

great pause and thought to the caseworker who too frequently is exclusively identified with his own culture.

The very use of the word *foreign* here is illustrative of our prejudiced attitudes. Although it is put in italics to point up the fact that any culture that represents a difference is considered foreign, it is well to be explicit about this. The Hawaiians are the natives. The Americans, Portuguese, Chinese are the foreigners. In the United States our own Indians are treated as if they represent a foreign culture. Foreign and different have become unfortunately synonymous.

It is significant that the caseworkers in Mrs. Handley's book were all persons who had some background and personal experience with different cultures. Themselves subjected to and undoubtedly aware of the conflict between cultures, they were ready to offer more than lip service to their respect for the individual differences of their clients. This identifying aspect of their relationship with these people in trouble undoubtedly was an important factor in their ability to be helpful.

Mrs. Handley details the record of the Kamuela family,* who had been receiving assistance under the Aid to Dependent Children Program for ten years following Mr. Kamuela's death from leprosy. The record was replete with workers' frustration due to ten years of lack of cooperation on the part of Mrs. Kamuela. The new worker began by reversing the criticism of former workers for Mrs. Kamuela's frequent moves and distribution of the children and various relatives. He recognized this as part of the Hawaiian pattern of communal responsibility. He was then able to enlist Mrs. Kamuela's cooperation in discussing the eldest daughter's problem.

*Ibid. p 6.

Alice, soon to be 18 and cut off from ADC, was reported to be ill but was kept in hiding. Having established a cooperative relationship with Mrs. Kamuela, the worker could finally ask whether Mrs. Kamuela's hesitation was related to the possibility that Alice had leprosy like her father. Sobbing with anxiety and relief, Mrs. Kamuela admitted this was so. Alice was tired of hiding and desired hospitalization. Mrs. Kamuela, however, still believed in the *Kahuna,* a Hawaiian specialist in nature knowledge.

The caseworker did not scoff at what could easily be termed Mrs. Kamuela's superstitions. He listened with respect. But he also held firm to his (and Alice's) recognition of the need for more scientific medical care for Alice. Mrs. Kamuela also was aware of the conflict between the "old" customs, in which she truly believed, and the "new," which was the reality of her environment. But she was permitted to have her "different" feelings.

Cultural factors also can be represented in the social milieu in which a particular client lives and functions. A young girl, Mary G., from a typically white, Protestant, middle-class, midwestern farm family, came to a large city. She quickly found a job, made friends, began dating and superficially made an excellent adjustment. However, she was aware that she was consistently finding the "wrong kind of boy friends." She thought she wanted to marry a warm, sympathetic young man, but she was constantly being caught up in one group after another where relationships were tenuous and sexual promiscuity was the way of life. This was distasteful to her. She brought in a long story one day of how she had gone to a restaurant with her roommate. There was a friendly atmosphere in the place. Several people waiting at the bar for their table had suggested a party after dinner. The two girls went and were horrified to find that the party included shared sexual intercourse. Questioning revealed that the restaurant was in a neighborhood frequented by expensive prostitutes; such "parties" were the customary procedure. Mary hesitantly admitted that she "had heard" about this particular neighborhood. Actually it was notorious in the city. Mary had thought of moving here with her girlfriend. There were many "respectable" people living here too. Her exaggerated interest in sex and long-repressed curiosity became apparent. The worker's awareness of the mores of this neighborhood helped clarify more quickly Mary's conflict. She was so curious and basically so ignorant about sex that she was drawn to sexually acting-out groups "in order to learn." Again the unconscious implications were apparent to the worker but were not interpreted. Instead, clarification of the milieu Mary was seeking, sharpened the focus of treatment. She was helped to secure scientific knowledge of sex and to ventilate some of her conscious fears and attitudes towards this as influenced by her farm background, where animal sexuality was obvious and in marked contrast to the attitude of her parents, who acted as if sex did not exist.

A dilemma that confronts all of us and cannot be resolved here also poses a problem for caseworkers. How much should behavior be changed by entering into the cultural pattern and how much can the cultural pattern be changed by casework invervention? A white school principal in a black ghetto achieved respect from his students and discipline in his school by unhesitatingly using physical punishment for infractions of school rules. He was a warm, friendly person who liked his pupils but knew that in his community physical force was an important factor in maintaining respect and authority. His slaps and spankings were considered fair in that culture.

The children were better-behaved. There were fewer dropouts in his school than in other ghetto schools. Some therapists of all disciplines are incorporating this in a reward-and-punishment theory of therapy. Shall caseworkers be transmitters of culture which is an adaptation to a harsh reality? Faced with a specific individual, which choice can he make? If he teaches a child the value of nonviolence and the child returns to live in a culture where violence is the gauge of status, has the caseworker been helpful?

Mary Richmond's astuteness and vision have often been extolled. There is no sound area of casework practice that cannot find corroboration in her work. What she has to say about Orientals in the following quotation applies equally to all cultures different from the culture of the caseworker and of the agency he represents:

> To our unaccustomed eyes, these Orientals look alike and seem alike, and we are betrayed by our ignorance into treating them alike. Any honest sharing of reality with them would bring out immediately their individual differences, for with each examination into the details of their lives, social stratification would be washed away and the infinite diversity of gifts, of characteristics become apparent. Only after such a plunge has been made repeatedly, however, do we arrive at an even profounder truth; only then do we begin to realize in any complete sense the fundamental likeness of our human kind in their primary relations and experiences—in their struggles and mistakes, their need of guidance, their right to opportunity, to fuller development, to diversity.*

*Ibid. in preface.

Conclusion

The culture of the society in which the child is reared and lives affects the development of every individual. The caseworker needs to be alert to those cultural and environmental differences that help explain the dynamic pattern of the client's emotional functioning. It is also imperative for the caseworker to be aware of how cultural differences affect the way in which reality is perceived. Lack of this awareness can influence the worker to set up unrealistic goals for his client. It may also set up barriers of misunderstanding that would vitiate and frustrate any attempt on the part of the caseworker to be helpful. The caseworker should also be aware of the many subcultures within any society, as demonstrated by neighborhoods or economic class. Discussion with the client of these cultural differences is often essential to the establishment of a relationship of fundamental mutual respect.

Chapter Seven

Recording

Recording is an essential part of social casework treatment. All workers accept it in theory but rebel in practice. It is recognized as important, and experienced as irksome. More and more, caseworkers are evaluating the benefits of detailed recording when balanced against the administrative expense involved in recording the service.

There are times when detailed recording is invaluable, especially for research or teaching purposes. Tape recorders are becoming popular and useful in these instances. But, like any other new custom, they are frequently used indiscriminately and often do not justify their use. Tapes, recording machines and the storage costs of both, add to the expense budgets of clinics and agencies. Dictating machines and secretaries also are increasing in cost. The essential function of a social agency is service to the community. This must take precedence. A full verbatim recording can only be justified by a sound rationale.

With consistent emphasis on the diagnostic thinking and orientation of caseworkers, recording of an interview will represent the distillation of the true process of the session rather than a retelling of the events in the actual words. Such a summary would include: (1) meaningful data from the client; (2) movement backward, forward or status quo in treatment; (3) affect of the client; (4) activity of both worker and client; and (5) emotional interaction between the two. Obviously there is much overlapping of these areas. In some instances, one sentence will answer all four criteria.

Recording of intake interviews, with their heavy emphasis on essential factual information, will necessarily be longer than the recording of the interviews that follow. The stage of development of the worker, the worker's individual manner of expression, his certainty in the treatment of the individual client, will all influence the length of the recording. As indicated previously, the administrative policy of the agency and the consequent goals of treatment will also affect the kind of material to be selected or omitted. The goal, however, would be to extract the treatment process from the interview. What did the worker contribute? What did the client contribute? What was the significance of the interview? In what way was the progress of treatment hindered or stimulated, and why? Recording of this type might be done interview by interview, or in a summary of several interviews. Hopefully, the choice would be determined by the movement in the treatment rather than by the worker's inclination to make time in his busy schedule for dictation.

This selective type of recording, based on a diagnostic approach to casework treatment, is truly process recording—describing the process, not just a record of the interview from which the reader can extract the process that occurred. The affect, the interrelationship, the content significant during the interview or important for future references—all find their place in this more descriptive type of recording. An eyewitness account from which the astute reader may glean what actually transpired is far more concealing than condensed recording which emphasizes the diagnostically oriented treatment process.

Every worker will have clients, or particular interviews or parts of an interview, that he will want to record in detail. These are useful for periods of thoughtful application of hindsight, so that at a later date he may find out for himself or with the aid of his supervisor or consultant what happened and why it puzzled him. By and large, the very act of distillation frequently clarifies the puzzle. The thoughtfulness that produces condensed recording is indicative of the thoughtfulness that was present before, during and after an interview. In the process of thinking through what happened during an interview, the caseworker will frequently gain an insight into what has taken place, if he was not already aware of it. The worker who is thinking diagnostically can record the results of an interview in a few lines or a paragraph or two.

Good casework treatment implies a specific focus. All interpretations are geared to the focus and to the relationship between worker and client. The recording is a diary of the progress in the client's developing self-awareness and his ability to use the therapeutic relationship. The deviations from the focus that occur but are not dealt with in the interview, will be briefly noted. The need to distill an interview into a diagnostically oriented, condensed entity, helps to stimulate the acuity of a worker during an interview and make him more keenly aware of the actual process as it takes place.

The type of recording naturally varies with the nature of treatment. Both are influenced by administrative policy. If the worker listens to the client with emphasis on remembering or noting what is being said in order to transmit it verbatim to a record, he is apt to be less alert to the significance of the material. If, however, the worker is thinking throughout the interview of how the material presented by the client is furthering or hindering progress toward the treatment goal, that worker's attitudes and responses during the interview will be more disciplined. Training in this type of recording clarifies the treatment process, helps sharpen the worker's skills and helps make interpretations more meaningful and timely.

This diagnostically oriented recording often places more responsibility on the memory of the worker for factual details. This, too, is a valuable asset. Verbal material presented in supervisory conferences, supplementing the written records, can be far more revealing to worker and supervisor of what actually took place than a verbatim report. What is omitted, what is temporarily forgotten, as well as what is recorded, is a good indication of the worker's understanding and progress. Full recording, other than on tapes, is no assurance that omissions will be unimportant. On the contrary, they are frequently the most important "missing link."

Obviously such a method, like all other aspects of casework treatment, should be used flexibly and adapted to the needs of the client and the practitioner. That part of an interview in which the details illustrate most pointedly some attitude or conflict of a client should be included verbatim. It is equally true that a direct quotation often tells more about the client and the process than any description.

It must be remembered that a case record is in the files for a particular purpose. First, it is a record of treatment to date for review and consideration by the worker. Secondly, it is a record for possible staff consideration, case study meetings, supervision, or consultation. Thirdly, it is a record in preparation for possible transfer to another worker. It must therefore be intelligible to a colleague as well as to the caseworker. Fourthly, it may be an administrative device for essential recordkeeping. Recording for research purposes might necessarily have a different focus.

The following is an extract from an interview recorded for presentation at a seminar in a clinic. The client is an obsessive neurotic who at this point in treatment is concerned primarily with his feelings about masturbation and his continued use of unnecessary medication for his eyes.

"Patient was 20 minutes late because he was a little late getting out of work. He told me that he had had no drops in his eyes since Saturday. He put them in once Saturday morning and then could tolerate it no longer; he was using the last of the bottle of drops and felt that if he bought another bottle he would be tied down for three months more. He called his doctor and told him he was disgusted, and the doctor told him to stop for two months and then have his eyes examined again. However, all weekend he was greatly disturbed, since he used the drops only once on Saturday. Perhaps he should have put them in the four times Saturday and then stopped on Sunday. He was uncomfortable all weekend. This morning he felt so uncomfortable that he had to call his mother and tell her that he was under such tension that he didn't know what to do with himself. He finally lived through the time when he could call his doctor and get reassurance from him and then felt very foolish, but better. All weekend, he had a feeling of foreboding about having stopped the drops, and yet a feeling of relief at not having to put the drops in and worry about them all the time, but he was unable to explain the feeling of foreboding. I suggested that it might have some relation to the thing we had talked about last week —that putting in the drops had been a kind of shield for himself from activity that was difficult. I pointed out that we do not get rid of feelings as quickly as we can accept them intellectually. Patient accepted this idea quite readily, but did not pursue it.

"Another thing that disturbed him this morning was that two people made disparaging remarks about him and he took them too seriously. He knows one was jesting; he still is not certain about the other. One of his fellow employees said something to him about being unshaven and when patient showed that he was sensitive about it, this fellow immediately said he was joking, that many people were unable to take a close shave. Patient shaves only every other day because his skin is so sensitive. Then, later, when he was getting on the elevator, the operator said something to him about being a dope fiend, a narcotic addict. Patient felt then that he was worrying so much about his drops that he was beginning to look old and haggard. In addition to that, one of the sales clerks had asked him during the morning whether he was feeling ill, because he looked as if he had something on his mind. Patient constantly worries about growing old. I wondered if these remarks could be related to his feeling that he was growing old. Patient knows that other people think he looks much younger than he is and this pleases him a great deal. If anyone ever remarked that he looked older he would worry. I said we all had a resistance to growing up and facing additional responsibilities, and patient felt that this had a lot to do with his fear. He has never had to be on his own. He could always, in an emergency, turn to his parents for help. He does not know whether he could manage on his own, but also, in this, is his fear of not look-ing well. If he is young-looking and fresh-looking, he believes that people will like him better. Patient related this to his old guilt about masturbation. He always felt that when he masturbated he looked haggard and worn and then people would not like him. In response to my question, he said he never thought people would think badly of him because he masturbated, because he always had known that everybody masturbated. All his guilt was illogical and unaccountable. He never thought that other people would accuse him of it, but did feel that people did not like him because he did something that made him look bad. He is still surprised to recognize that he could feel guilty about something he knew was nor-mal. He used to walk down the street and when other people would look at him, he would feel that they were looking at him with distaste. Now, when he walks down the street and people look at him, he feels that they are looking at him admiringly. He feels that some of this is due to the fact that he has more friends now. He is well-liked at the store; the other boys accept him as one of them. They fool around with him, slapping him on the back, giving him playful punches, and so on. Also, the boy downstairs whom he had always wanted as a friend, but who never showed too much interest in him, is now inviting him to come in and suggesting things they do together. Also, he is going to the recreation center more often and is beginning to make friends there."

Condensed for the record, it reads as follows:

"Patient was delayed at work and was 20 minutes late. He has stopped using the eye drops but felt great anxiety about whether he should have stopped. This morning the anxiety was so intense he had to telephone mother from the job just to tell her about it until he could get the proper reassurance from the doctor. This was related to the previous interpretation of symptoms as a defense against individual responsibility and patient agreed. Two casual, unflattering comments about patient's appearance made him worry again about growing old. Patient related this to dependence on parents and fear of accepting adult responsibility, as well as to guilt about masturbation, which he used to feel was self-damaging. This used to make him feel that people looked upon him with disfavor but his present improved social relations have reversed this. Although the patient associated his need to be dependent to his guilt about masturbation, he avoided recognition of this."

The condensed version gives: (1) the patient's progress in therapy: he stopped using the eye drops but developed anxiety; (2) the interpretation of the therapist and the patient's reaction; (3) patient's use of a previous interpretation to demonstrate his growing insight into his patterns of behavior.

Series of Condensed Interviews

The next illustration is a series of interviews to show how meaningful a continuous case record, using condensed recording exclusively, can be.

This is the case of a 26-year-old married man, immature and dependent, with marked schizoid trends. His presenting symptoms were some depression and anxiety. These were first precipitated by his brother's imprisonment by the enemy. Both boys had been reared in a constantly competitive situation by numerous foster parents. The mother died when the patient was an infant; the father had been a traveling salesman. When both boys returned from service, they joined the father in a small business. The latter was an irascible, demanding person who set impossibly high standards for the patient in his business.

Interview 1

"Patient was very tired. He had had a very bad night. He still does not remember what he dreams about. His wife wakes him up when he starts to scream but he cannot remember what it is or what precipitated the nightmare. We talked about this in terms of the patient's bad feelings being too difficult to fight under any circumstance. Patient agreed that this might be part of his trouble. I commented that patient had told me only good things about his father and brother. Despite the fact that he loves them so much, he was certain to have bad feelings about them too. Patient hesitated, seemed a little taken aback about this, but he agreed that it might be true. Now that he thinks of it, when he does get angry at his father or brother he has to pass it off as a joke for fear of how this bad feeling might overwhelm him."

Interview 2

"For the first time and only with considerable help was patient able to articulate his despondency over his overwhelming feeling of inadequacy in face of the responsibility of the business. He never had this much responsibility before and while he thinks he is a good businessman, his father can do much better and patient feels he should be able to do as well as father. He knows he is better than brother at learning business but frequently wishes he could go out into the hills and not be bothered by anybody or anything for awhile. I agreed that it was a difficult responsibility to be "shoved" upon someone so suddenly. Patient told me that he had not had a real rest after his discharge from service; he used his vacation to go back east for a visit. If he would like a vacation now, his father would be glad to arrange it, but he does not feel it is fair to ask the father. In the near future, they hope to be able to employ a manager for the store and patient will then be given another store. In between, he will try to get a vacation. He talked also of his feelings of responsibility toward his expected child. Patient states he thinks of this often and with pleasure. His only concern is that the baby be healthy and his wife have no difficulty."

Interviews 3 and 4

"With great feeling, patient talked of his guilt in relation to his brother, which started when he was young. He feels this has been all-pervasive and has kept him from expressing his feelings to his family and made him more irritable with people outside his family. Many little feelings have piled up which he feels account in great part for his depression. Patient planned to try to change this but we recognized together that this would be difficult and in the second interview patient accepted the fact that it was difficult but it was something he was learning to do. Patient related his feelings of inadequacy to the fact that as a child he got a lot of love and attention which he thought he did not deseve. Equally, he got the store without any investment of his own while his brother put in several thousand dollars which he had gotten from his in-laws. Father had put in his money. Therefore, patient once more had taken a great deal without putting in anything of his own, and he was feeling guilty as a result. This was a repetition of his previous pattern."

The value of these interviews lies in the patient's

growing ability to recognize the relationships of his feelings of inadequacy and guilt to his repressed anger and to his symptoms. The recording emphasizes his movement from the hesitant reaction to the interpretation in the first interview to spontaneous verbalizations in the third. The many incidents that the patient related to prove his points would not add anything to our understanding of him or his progress; for example, the many times he withheld anger to his father and mother; the details of his responsibilities in the business; the illustrations of the times in his childhood when he received love he did not deserve.

In any agency where transfer of clients from one worker to another is minimal and the sole purpose of recording is to serve as a base for recollection for the worker and perhaps a guide to the supervisor or consultant, all four of the interviews could be summarized as follows:

"Mr. Z. moved gradually from an intellectual acceptance with reservation of worker's interpretation of the anger underlying his depression to spontaneous expressions of guilt about being favored above his brother. He ventilated his feelings of guilt and his ambivalence about the responsibilities thrust upon him soon after discharge from service. He expressed only pleasure in anticipation of his forthcoming child. This was not pursued at this time. He moved from expression of guilt to association with his feelings of inadequacy and resulting depression."

Teaching Considerations

The use of diagnostically condensed recording can be valuable in the teaching process. The beginning worker is asked to record this interview in the traditional detailed manner or almost verbatim. The supervisory conference focuses on what was important in the interview and the reasons for its importance. It has been found that the process of verbalizing the dynamics of the interview helps the student emphasize for himself the movement or lack of progress in treatment, and the reasons for either. The diagnostic recording after the conference then becomes an important tool in the integration of learning. The final dictation is of help to the supervisor in evaluating the results of the supervisory conference.

The following is a new worker's first summary of an hour's interview—her first with this particular patient following an intake interview by another worker. In the intake, it was learned that this 24-year-old single man was attending engineering school. His chief complaint was the frequency of explosive outbursts, of temper, especially with women. There was a history of extreme rejection and restriction by his mother and stepfather and rivalry with an older, more favored brother. The patient had a great drive for accomplishment and had achieved the rank of sergeant in the Army. He also complained of occasional depression and feelings of tension.

The worker was new to the clinic but had had some previous experience in social agencies. Her first record of her interview was three and a half pages long and was almost a verbatim account, although some effort had been made to be selective. Lack of space forbids its reproduction. The worker was asked to try to analyze the interview diagnostically and to record it briefly.

"Patient talked at a slow pace, with long pauses before statements. In explaining why he had not come for treatment sooner, he mentioned having given up going with girls at all for a while, and that he continued to have trouble when he did resume contact. After deciding to seek help, he had postponed actually coming to the clinic for a long time.

"Most of the interview was devoted to exploring the situations in which he blew up, patient giving three examples. The first concerned an occasion when a girl used vulgar language, a characteristic patient considers unbecoming to nice girls. The second referred to an incident when a girl 'teased him,' that is, when he wasn't taken seriously and what he said was questioned. Patient has strong feelings about always telling the truth and expects people to believe him. A third example related to his attempt to 'get fresh' with the girl he is going with now. When she resisted him, he went into a sulking spell and threatened to quit going with her, although he says he wouldn't have respected her had she permitted him to go ahead. He doesn't attribute his reaction to denial of sexual intercourse because he used to blow up with an army nurse with whom he did have intercourse.

"This nurse had suggested that he really needed someone to love him and care for him. In order to avoid becoming involved with her he had been 'mean' to her, the most effective way of hurting her being for him to belittle himself. Patient is impatient with himself for his behavior at these times but cannot seem to control his reaction on the next occasion.

"The only animation shown by the patient occurred when he was told that his score on the intelligence test was above average. This precipitated discussion of his interest in psychology and of his admiration for a female psychology teacher he had had, the only positive relationship with a woman of which he had spoken. He acceded readily to request that he take a Rorschach test and an appointment was given him."

In the supervisory conference, discussion centered around the worker's role in the interview and her confusion about the goal in treatment. What was her understanding of the man's problem and what was the man demonstrating? The value of having the worker write a summary before the supervisory conference might be open to discussion. Whether verbal conferences preceding dictation, should be a device more frequently used, is a matter that deserves attention. The summary reproduced above was actually recorded and formed the basis for the supervisory conference.

It was noted that the worker left herself out of the record entirely. This stimulated discussion of the importance of the worker-client relationship and the worker's responsibility for progress. The second point was the difference between what the man said and the meaning of his statements. This second summary followed the supervisory conference:

"Patient waited for me to begin. I raised the question of his delay in seeking treatment. Patient expressed his fear of being "a little bit off" and delaying treatment until a recent repetition of his explosive outburst with his current girlfriend.

"Patient then began to talk spontaneously but with long pauses. Encouraged to talk about specific incidents, he told of reacting to his girl's use of 'vulgar language' and to being teased and not taken seriously. He also told of using his explosiveness to hurt his previous girlfriend and thus end the relationship. He verbalized guilt about these outbursts. I said it would be our goal in working together to help him understand his reactions and learn to cope with these situations.

"When he was told that the psychological test showed him to be above average in intelligence, he spoke with great warmth of a positive relationship with an older woman who expressed confidence in him."

As the worker and supervisor evaluated this man's behavior in terms of what it meant—his feelings of inadequacy and his resultant fear of relationships—the focus of future treatment became more manifest.

Economy of words, plus an accurate record of the patient's personality patterns and the dynamics of treatment must be the keynote of any good recording. The more thoughtful and discriminating the selection of material, the better will be the record and the service to the client and patient.

Conclusion

The recording of diagnostic casework treatment follows closely the lines of the treatment itself. In other words, it is the thread of the therapeutic process, which follows logically from intake to termination, that is entered into the record. Exceptions from the central theme may be noted or ignored according to their diagnostically determined value. Exceptions will also be made, necessarily, to accommodate research goals or administrative necessities. Generally, the greater the amount of thought, the more condensed and meaningful will be the recording.

Chapter Eight

Adolescents and Schizophrenics

The combination of adolescents and schizophrenics as a single group requiring special treatment techniques and procedures may seem strange. Actually they are quite different in the way they present themselves. There is no question that disturbed adolescents respond to treatment more quickly. Their basic ego structures are stronger and their drives towards maturity and health are greater. However, there are similarities. Perhaps the most striking similarity is the need of both groups for realistic parents who are loving, indulgent, but firm and consistent. In both these instances, the caseworker must be free to assume the dual responsibility of therapist and parent. The caseworker must not be fearful of the essential authority that every good parent must reserve for himself. Both disturbed adolescents and schizophrenics are hostile to authority. They mistrust it. Each group may express its hostility in different ways for different reasons. But both these groups of people are essentially looking for the love which breeds self-respect. They are searching for a model for identification purposes. They

119

are begging for an adult to set limits within which they can establish their own identities. The adolescent who comes for treatment is naturally in a process of flux and change. The schizophrenic has tried and feels he has failed. The anxious adolescent truly has not had any experience in the adult world and may be fearful, uncertain and unknowledgeable about it. The schizophrenic has usually had experiences in the adult world that were traumatic and frightening. But, surprisingly enough, he is usually equally uncertain and unknowledgeable because of the extent of his distortion.

The major difference that distinguishes these two groups from the other myriad kinds of individuals who are clients in social agencies is their need for a parent. With both these individuals, the casework relationship and the caseworker's use of himself in relationship to these clients is of paramount importance. Often the focus of insight shifts frequently. But the constant focus is usually the development and strengthening of the client's ego. The caseworker, more than in any other therapeutic relationship, is the teacher and guide through and to the adult world of reality. He may get angry; he may be more open about his interest, affection and approval. He is the parent surrogate, and any attempt on the part of the caseworker to try to withdraw from this role will inevitably be disruptive to the treatment. This does not mean that excessive dependency is encouraged. Like any good parent, the caseworker's goal is the independence of the client. Like any good parent, the caseworker is proud of his child's ability to leave the parental protection and stand on his own two feet securely.

Both types of clients almost always require collateral interviews with parents. Unless one or both parents are in some type of therapy, it is usually most helpful for the same caseworker who is treating the adolescent or schizophrenic, to see the relatives. The younger the client, the more frequent may be the interviews with parents. But even the older adolescent and the ambulatory schizophrenic need this kind of environmental support. Probably the only exceptions would be the schizophrenic client who is not living with parents or parent-surrogates, but is living alone. This, however, is a rather unusual circumstance, at least at the beginning of casework treatment. It is the nature of the conflict of both these groups of individuals, that dependency is a marked characteristic. Both are tied to adult authoritative figures in a deeply hostile manner which is only reinforced by their dependency needs.

Who is seen first, parent or prospective client, is frequently determined by circumstance. A parent may request help and only at intake reveal that he is seeking help for a son or daughter. Or the parent may be so blocked that he is unable to know how to present, to the prospective client, the agency, clinic or social worker as a resource. The parent often needs concrete advice and counseling in this beginning phase. If the emphasis is to be on the adolescent or schizophrenic, the parent can be given some educational background of how individuals like these usually behave. They should be prepared for the probable stormy rebellious periods ahead. They should also be advised of their rights to react as human beings. Their personalities are the realities that the client is going to have to learn to live with. Some of the parents' hostility towards the client can be ameliorated by intellectual understanding. The burden of deeper understanding is going to fall on the client. But the knowledge that the person who is treating the more obviously disturbed individual understands that the parents are having a difficult time too, is often of benefit to all. Both adolescents and schizophrenics must be told that parents will be seen. They must be assured that no confidence will be broken. They will know in advance what the caseworker intends to discuss with the parents. They will know in their next individual session what transpired. Parents, too, must be advised that the client will know all that takes place.

Joint sessions of adolescents or schizophrenics with the parents are extremely valuable assets if used discriminately. The client has an opportunity to test the reality of his reactions and has the support of the caseworker in expressing his hostilities directly to his parents. The worker must be cautious to schedule these interviews in accordance with the readiness of the client and the parents to accept them. Joint sessions that are not thoroughly planned can precipitate increased withdrawal or a mounting of hostility that becomes overwhelming and intolerable. In a hospital where the schizophrenic patient is removed from his family, there is less need to be cautious. There the hospital personnel are available to cushion the effect of disturbing family interviews. When the adolescent or ambulatory schizophrenic is living at home, the caseworker must be especially alert to what each of the persons involved is going to carry home and how this will affect the interaction within the family in the periods between sessions. This is far more true of these two groups whose relationships to the world outside themselves is still so tenuous and tentative.

Precisely because the caseworker does supplant the parent in both these instances, he must be on guard not to arouse even more hostility in them. Some parents are delighted to be relieved of the responsibility of being a parent. Thses are often quick to assert their own dependency needs. Unless these are obvious to the parent as well and treatment referral is made for parents, they can be met by direct guidance: "Johnny needs to be told to go to school." "At this time permit him to stay in bed a little longer in the morning." "Don't nag him to eat; do encourage him to eat." The advice must be geared to the reality needs of both client and parent at any particular time. This is also a way of enlisting the help of the parent and making him a partner in the enterprise of helping the client "get well."

If the client has come for help without consulting his parents, the reasons for seeing them must be clarified with the client first. The focus in these sessions with the parents will probably then be on hearing them out, giving them an opportunity to ventilate their grievances and thus engaging them in the helping process. It must always be clear to all concerned that as long as the client lives with his family, they will all be involved in his disturbances in one way or another.

The controlling, domineering parent is equally destructive and hostile. But he too is the object of equally hostile behavior from the client. The caseworker must be aware that such a parent is even more threatened by having to trust his child, no matter how old, to a stranger. The caseworker, no matter how his skill is recognized, is still a stranger intruding into an intimate, troubled family situation. Recognition of this, even if only on an intellectual basis, with both parents and client is essential.

The adolescent period is naturally one of turmoil The adolescent is subject to many pressures, physiological and emotional, social and familial. He is reaching out to break the tie to his parents and frequently overdoes it. This still within normal limits. He is attempting to establish and integrate his own standards of morality, of society, of his own goals for himself. A certain amount of confusion is again realistic for his stage of development. He is caught between the pleasures of being a child with minimal responsibilities and the gratifications of being an adult primarily responsible to and for himself. One mother described her adolescent daughter as being in a hurry to wear high heels and play with dolls. The adolescent has a great need to consolidate his position with his peers. In this way, he is greatly different from the ambulatory schizophrenic. The sexual awareness of himself and the opposite sex is heightened, and the adolescent's clumsiness is often disturbing to him. The frequent confusion of heterosexual and homosexual drives, not openly recognized but felt as disturbing, can form the background for other more overt disturbances. Adolescence is a period of reliving in a heightened form the basic aggression, self-assertion, fear of dependency of infancy and latency, plus an uncertainty as to what is male and what is female. Adolescence is an age where the child's maturation may stimulate anxiety in an insecure parent. This in turn provokes greater conflict in the child. This parental uncertainty increases the strain on the developing ego of the adolescent, since he is offered no guide lines. He turns to his peers but often finds only more uncertainty and reinforcement of his conflicts. The adolescent may need only an authoritative but kindly figure to "talk things out," or he may need more intensive attention to his conflicts and his ongoing organization or defensive patterns. The neurotic adolescent in this sense is like the schizophrenic because he, too, is overwhelmed by his reality and is groping. They are both mistrustful because they are hurt and feel so very vulnerable. Both are bewildered by a need for and lack of comprehension of their lack of omnipotence. The "sharing" aspects of casework treatment have even greater value for both these kinds of clients. They have to learn to share and to trust in a way others may have learned at least partially before coming for help. Both adolescent and schizophrenic are equally confused about why they are not liked more by the adults around them. They feel they have disappointed all the important adults in their lives and feel very isolated. "No one understands me" is the frequent cry of even the "normal" adolescent. The intensity of this cry is terrifying for the disturbed adolescent and the schizophrenic alike.

The schizophrenic who is treated by social workers not employed by state mental hospitals is usually ambulatory, nonhallucinatory, living a marginal kind of existence. We are not here concerned with the totally withdrawn and isolated individual who has to be hospitalized and have the environmental therapeutic atmosphere that is implied in this need for hospitalization. Because social work training is so firmly founded on the caseworker's knowledge of himself in relationship to others, it is to casework that psychiatrists frequently turn for help for these schizophrenics. The schizophrenic is an emotionally retarded and deprived individual who is yearning for a love he never had and yet is so fearful of that love that he thwarts every effort made to fulfill any part of that yearning. No one can ever give the schizophrenic all that he desires. Like the developing child, he must learn to tolerate frustration, recognizing slowly little by very little that this time the frustration comes from the demands of a positive loving reality, not from hostility or withholding. This takes time and patience, and the worker and the agency must be prepared to give both unstintingly at first and in decreasing doses in proportion to the schizophrenic's developing ego. It should be noted here that schizophrenics like neurotics have differing capacities. Consequently different levels of achievement can be expected of each individual. It is important to set many goals, one at a time, each one only a little further from the previous goal. For example, just keeping appointments regularly each week can sometimes be a first goal and an indication of trust. The frequency of appointments is regulated by the need and capacity of the client. Some schizophrenics can only tolerate interviews once a week, or once every two weeks. Some are so close to a complete break with reality that they may need several interviews a week with the privilege of reaching the caseworker by telephone between sessions.

From time to time, a schizophrenic who is untreatable is referred to a social agency. At intake they are indistinguishable from those who can and do respond to treatment. There are no psychological tests yet devised to distinguish them. No one who is aware of this problem has been able to isolate them. Therapists who have worked with many schizophrenics over a long period of time seem to "sense" when a client or patient is "untreatable." And here, of course, we must always question how much of this "sense" of untreatability is communicated to the patient. There have been instances where such an individual was treated by someone else who did believe in his treatability, and the client still did not respond. For the most part, however, schizophrenics are treatable. Given enough time, they respond most positively to treatment and eventually can live satisfying and rewarding lives that are satisfying and rewarding to themselves and are a contribution to the community in which they live. How far they can develop into marital partners and parents is again highly variable. How much this is related to early deprivation and how much to a "constitutional" factor is still an interesting question for research and exploration.

Always remembering and allowing for the important factor of individual differences, the kinds of resistance to relationship presented by adolescents and schizophrenics constitutes an important diagnostic criterion. The adolescent is fearful of authority because in his emotional distortion authority represents infantilism. He is therefore frequently hostile out of rebellion. His rebellion takes the form of broken appointments, challenge of the caseworker's interpretation, constant testing of the caseworker to determine how much freedom he will be permitted to have and not to have. The worker's respect for the adolescent's need to be rebellious, his willingness to give the adolescent the right to make choices at the same time that the caseworker holds firmly to his delineation of reality all combine to dissipate the resistance. The adolescent is then helped to use his energies constructively for his own development.

The schizophrenic is fearful and hostile too. But his fear represents far more his mistrust of all human beings who ask more from him than he can give. The very closeness that the adolescent encourages in order to permit him to be rebellious, is horribly frightening to the schizophrenic. The latter usually needs a long period of learning very gradually that he can trust his own feelings. His resistance expresses this fear. His withdrawal is based on his inability to tolerate his own feelings. It is a seeming anomaly that the more positive the reaction of the schizophrenic is to the caseworker, the more fearful he may become. This must be acknowledged and respected by, for example, spacing the interviews at longer periods. The worker must freely permit distance and isolation until the schizophrenic builds up his tolerance for a relationship. Once a week, or once every two weeks is frequently all a schizophrenic can tolerate at the beginning of treatment. The fact that the relationship is tenuous does not imply that it is not real. Hopefully, the same caseworker should be available to the schizophrenic over the long period of years that treatment is necessary. This is even of greater importance to the schizophrenic than to the adolescent. It is of greater importance to the adolescent than to the neurotic. This does not mean that transfers do not affect the neurotic. The neurotic, with help, bounces back more quickly; at the other end of the scale is the schizophrenic who reacts with increased fear and mistrust, which takes a long time to resolve.

Finally it must be emphasized that this is not an attempt to delineate in detail the various multitude of differences presented in both categories of adolescents and schizophrenics. These are two types of clients who require more flexible use of the authority and consistent warmth of relationship.

Case I: The Adolescent

Georgianna M. was a 19-year-old girl when her parents "brought" her for treatment. She was a freshman in college. She was bright and had achieved a fair amount of success as an artist and musician. Now suddenly she was getting poor grades at school and, worst of all, was associating with undesirable men, "like Jews and beatniks." Mr. M. made it quite clear in the first interview that he wanted to be certain the caseworker was not a Communist. He had heard all about the liberal tendencies of social workers. Mrs. M. just wept and talked about all that had been done for "Georgie." They were not very wealthy but could well afford to give Georgie all that she wanted, and they had done so. All Mrs. M. wanted was to have Georgie happy. She seemed to be aware that Georgianna's dating might be an acting-out of rebellion primarily against a rigid father. She was most grateful for the worker's acknowledgment of this. Mr. M. was told that the worker agreed that probably Georgianna's choice of friends represented some unhealthy conflict, but that he had to be prepared for a continued acting-out of this behavior for some time before any change would be apparent. Both parents were assured that they could call to discuss this at any time that Georgianna's behavior became too difficult to tolerate.

Georgianna herself was seen the next day. She was aware of what had gone on in the interview with her parents. Mother always told her everything. Her parents had been having differences of opinion for some time. Mother used Georgianna as a confidante, continuously reassuring her that these differences did not matter very much since "Daddy and Mommy" loved each other so very much. Georgianna's first question, then, was to ask that the worker call her "Annie." She much preferred the feminine part of her name. When this was accepted, she was free to talk about her problems. She herself was very much concerned about her sudden lack of interest in school. She was also troubled about her relationship to her parents. They had always been so kind and loving, and now her father was so openly critical, and her mother, while verbalizing understanding, looked so martyred and pained. Her interest in "beatniks" was exaggerated. She had joined a more liberal and progressive church than that of her family. Here she had become acquainted with the group of which her father disapproved. He also was highly critical of the minister who had been the subject of some publicity in the local highly conservative press to which her father subscribed religiously. The particular boy she was dating at the moment, Art, was Jewish. She was aware that her father was not entirely wrong in being suspicious of Art: he had an irresponsible past, was a drifter, and would probably not make a good husband; but he was sympathetic and enjoyed folk music, as did Annie, and he was the only boy who showed any interest in her at this time. Annie was a very attractive young girl who managed to dress in a manner deliberately concealing her beauty. She looked severe and prim and isolated. It was easy to understand her lack of friends.

Annie was encouraged to give her own history. She was the oldest of five children, all of whom had been excessively indulged. She was her father's favorite. She could not understand how this pattern of quarreling had developed between them. It seemed to have started when she was about 14 or 15. Her mother had tried to act as conciliator, and Annie had tried to follow mother's advice. After all, this was the only time mother had ever asked anything of her. But she could not seem to conciliate father, nor could mother, really. The worker noted a tone of bitterness in the previous sentence. Asked about it, Annie burst into tears. No one had ever asked anything of her. Everything she had ever done had been just fine. Whether she had received C's or A's, she had been given the same approval. How was she to know what to do? Everything, anything, was always fine until now.

Annie had gone to this new church with her mother. She had been impressed with the conviction and sincerity of the minister and had become a regular member of the church. Mother usually accompanied her to services. This was the first time mother had done anything without father. Now, of course, she would discontinue her attendance. Annie would retain her membership in defiance of father. It was apparent that the minister, young and forthright and intellectually stimulating, was replacing father for Annie. Father had become too sexually stimulating. Both father and Annie were retreating in mutual panic, substituting their provocative quarrelsomeness for their unconscious sexual attraction. Because of the father's struggle with his own repressions, it was felt inadvisable to have joint sessions with Annie and her parents. Mother's masochistic support of father offered Annie no safe shelter in her own household. This then became the primary focus in treatment.

Annie was first helped to see that her failing in school was the result of much preoccupation with sexual fantasy. She was told directly that fathers frequently are attracted to their daughters and vice versa, and must learn to give up these yearnings and substitute more realistic expectations. The early interviews centered around her fantasies, her guilt about masturbation and the need to control these in order to stay in school. She wanted to become a teacher and had to learn to impose a certain amount of discipline on herself in order to achieve her own goals. One weekend, the father became so violent about Annie's dating that it almost seemed as though it might be necessary to consider hospitalization for him. He recovered quickly, remembered the conversation with the caseworker and requested another interview to ventilate his guilt. He was so fearful of another incident that he easily agreed to the worker's suggestion that he permit Annie to move to the dormitory of the college she was attending. This relieved a great deal of the tension between the two, and Annie was freer to concentrate more and more on her studies.

Living in the dormitory also brought Annie into closer social contact with her fellow students. On her weekends and holidays at home, she brought with her, friends of whom her parents could more realistically approve. With the caseworker's interviews as her safety-valve, she no longer needed Art. As her friends increased, her opportunities for sexual acting-out increased proportionately. She was constantly confused as to how this happened and why her quick sexual involvement seemed to sow the seeds for an end to a relationship. Again the worker stepped in authoritatively. Annie was getting herself into trouble, and for the present she had to avoid all possibilities of sexual involvement. She had to learn to relate to men as friends and companions before she could enjoy them as sexual partners. Annie could accept this as another step in learning self-discipline. She brought in many sexual fantasies and recognized over and over again how stimulated she had been by her father. She finally learned to give these up and to substitute shared pleasures other than sexual. She became active in a hiking club; she enjoyed swimming and tennis, as well as music and art. Her dating became more extensive, and she graduated from college with fairly good grades. She had made realistic plans to continue living away from home and maintain herself by her teaching. A year later, she telephoned to report that her parents had been killed in an accident. She was engaged to be married and she had many problems regarding the estate and her siblings. She was seen three times and it was clear to both Annie and the caseworker that she needed help only in integrating the shock of her parents' deaths. At one point, she said in tears, "This is so difficult. But the pain of separation from my parents now is nowhere as painful as the real separation from them in treatment. It is too bad we didn't have more time to enjoy each other once I learned to understand them and be tolerant of them."

Case II: The Schizophrenic

Polly F. was 22 when her mother sought help for her. She had made a not-too-serious suicidal attempt following an abortion, and the psychiatrist treating Polly in the hospital had made the referral. She was a sophomore in a college some distance away. The parents were bringing her home but wanted to arrange for treatment before she arrived. Mrs. F. was advised that Polly would have to be seen by the agency psychiatrist before a decision could be made as to whether or not Polly could be accepted for treatment. Mrs. F. was eager to agree to anything. She and Mr. F. would continue to support Polly as long as necessary. Mr. F. had a small business. Their income was uncertain, but they could always afford to give Polly a home and pay for her treatment.

Mrs. F. gave a brief history: Polly was the first of two children. She had been a very bright student, beloved by her parents and grandparents. She had been very pretty and received a great deal of attention from friends too. She was four when her brother was born. Mrs. F. had had a difficult second delivery and was ill for a year following the birth of Jerry. During this time, Polly had been placed in many foster homes, sometimes with the grand-parents, sometimes with foster parents found by a social agency. She had been a problem in all of these, and therefore had to be moved so frequently. The parents were reluctant to have her at home but did take her back when she was old enough to go to school. She did very well at school but was shy and retiring. She had few friends but was not much of a problem. When she went away to college, she suddenly gained a great amount of weight and began to associate with "peculiar" people. She became argumentative again, performed unevenly at school but managed to stay there. She had made it quite obvious to her parents that she was sexually promiscu-ous. As long as her college was some distance from home, the parents could "forget" Polly's troubles. They had felt so helpless. It seemed better that way. Now they could ignore Polly no longer. Jerry, the second child, was such an ideal child—not perfect, just "normal" and easy to handle. It was hard to understand. Mr. F. was an irascible man with an uneven temper. He was hard to predict. Perhaps that's where Polly's difficulties stemmed from. Mrs. F. was told that Polly could call for an appointment when she arrived. After a discussion with Polly, Mr. and Mrs. F. would be seen at least once again.

A week later, Polly came to the office by appointment. She was an extremely obese young woman with obvious beauty. She wore a huge tentlike coat despite the warm weather. Later she revealed that she rarely wore a dress so that she would not be tempted to take off her coat. She told the same story as that given by her mother but with much more feeling. She still felt deprived by not only being supplanted by her brother but being literally cast out of her home among strangers who showed little interest in her loneliness. She described her father's behavior in details which made clearer his seductive behavior with her when she was such "a pretty little girl." Her behavior at college was first provoked by once again being "thrown out" of the family enclave. She chose this college because of its scholastic standing and because she was becoming afraid of her father. He was constantly warning her of what men do to girls on dates and calling her nasty names, like "bitch" and "whore," if she stayed out too late. She felt that much of her acting-out was encouraged by her father. Like most schizophrenics, she was aware of much that might be unconscious in neurotic clients. Her friends at college were few, but they seemed to be a group of schizoid permanent undergraduates. They stayed in upper division by constantly changing majors. They clung to each other, relating by means of torrents of words, almost literally sharpening their wits on each other and by having sex with each other indiscriminately, with both males and females. Polly was dirty and unkempt. She had no plans for herself. She could not study or work. She was fearful of her parents' anger, and did not trust them. She spent most of her time daydreaming about becoming a movie star. When she could let go of her fat, she would be another Marilyn Monroe. The analogy was especially significant in view of Miss Monroe's well-publicized history of many ill-fated placements as a child. Polly's daydreams also included the love and attention she would automatically acquire once she could permit herself to become glamorous. Polly was seen by the agency psychiatrist, who agreed that the casework relationship was the procedure of choice. He felt—and psychological testing confirmed—that there was little, if any, danger of a repetition of the suicidal attempt. Polly herself had recognized this as a means of calling attention to her need for help.

Polly was seen by the caseworker for more than eight years. At first, she was seen three times weekly and then as the initial phase of panic subsided after almost eighteen months, the interviews varied from twice weekly to once every other week, depending on her activity in treatment and in reality. The first phase was the most critical. Her rebellion became flagrant. She continued her sexual promiscuity, including picking up men on street corners, but somehow managing to stay out of trouble with police and to avoid becoming pregnant.

During this phase of treatment, the worker established her role as the firm but accepting mother. Despite her rebellion and her insight into many aspects of her functioning, Polly was unaware of how angry she was and how frightened she was of this anger. Her fat and coat were not only protection for herself from people who could hurt her. They also helped keep her anger from getting out to destroy people, primarily her parents. During this stormy period, Polly would frequently call the social worker to threaten to leave town. She would be told firmly to return home, and later she would admit her need to test the worker's interest. Despite frequent interviews with the parents, separately and jointly, Polly's rebellion became too much for them, and they literally threw her out of the house. They decided they had done enough for the "ungrateful wretch." They did pay for her first month's rent in a furnished room but discontinued paying for her treatment at the agency. By this time, Polly had a part-time job as a waitress and could support herself minimally. During this phase, Polly continued her fantasies about her potential glamour and enrolled in a dramatic arts club at a recreation center. This group was too much for her, but she stayed on for the individual elocution lessons and used the group to seduce two of the men. Her relationships with men never lasted more than two or three nights at the most. Her homosexual relationships disappeared. The worker concentrated on keeping Polly employed and increasing her hours of employment. She was shown overt disapproval of her promiscuity as being of no benefit to herself and frequently a source of hurt, but as yet no prohibitions were set up.

In the second phase, Polly was encouraged to return to school to complete her degree. She was fearful and again often needed the authoritative firmness of the caseworker in order to continue. She did well scholastically but was both contemptuous and envious of her classmates. She decided to work for a teaching credential, feeling she understood children and could manage her relationships to them better than she could to adults. As her interest in her achievement increased and she ventilated more and more of her anger with her seductive father, her need for promiscuity decreased. Then the worker again asserted her authoritative role and prohibited further sexual activity for a while. Polly understood clearly the reasoning and timing behind this prohibition and agreed to it. It was understood that she would feel tempted and that she might slip, but that she had to learn this kind of discipline. There were no slips. This phase lasted through three years of college.

Upon graduation, Polly found a teaching job, and after the first few months of adjusting to a principal and other teachers on a professional level, she began to consider her extracurricular activities. Until now teaching had been a stopgap activity to keep her financially stable until she could lose enough weight to enable her to become a movie star. Now, with her learning to adjust to her peers in a professional milieu, she began to reexamine her goals for herself and to want to explore her problems of relating to friends, both male and female. With much advice and encouragement from the caseworker, she finally found the groups in her own intellectual level who could also function on a healthier emotional level of relationship. Throughout this period, Polly continued to have outbursts of anger towards her caseworker. Treatment was taking too long; it was the caseworker who was not helpful enough; or the worker would interrupt Polly's train of thought or would be provocative. The latter was a frequent accusation when Polly was reminded of her struggle with her fears and anxieties and the contribution of her fantasies to these. She continued to have many fantasies which had two primary themes: one, her success as a movie star with the world at her feet; two, overt sexual fantasies of hostile, castrating acts against the men of her acquaintance. In the final phase, first emphasis was placed on relieving Polly's guilt, the worker reiterating in one form or another, "fantasy is not reality." Secondly, her fantasies of hostility were related to her anger at her father and her expectation that all men were like her father. Thirdly, the comparison of glamour with the richness of everyday emotionally rewarding living, was rehearsed over and over. Finally, Polly was able to put herself on a diet after quarreling with the worker for not making loss of weight magically possible without effort on Polly's part. Then she began to date on a testing courtship basis and finally met a man towards whom she could freely express the tender feelings she had been so fearful of showing to anyone at first. This too began first with the caseworker, then to her friends, and finally to the man she expected to marry. During this period, too, she became friendly towards her parents and began to enjoy them for the limited companionship they could offer. Her brother, Jerry, began to show signs of desiring treatment, and Polly was most helpful and skillful in assisting him in resolving some of his initial resistances to applying to a psychiatric clinic.

The similarities between these two girls are striking. Yet Annie was not a schizophrenic, Polly was. Annie responded in less than four years; Polly took more than twice that long. Essentially that is the difference. Schizophrenics are more regressed than adolescents and need a longer period of nurturing and mothering (parenting?). It is a coincidence that both these girls chose to be teachers, each for a different reason: Annie wanted to use her art and music background in a secure, financially rewarding manner; Polly, because of her real interest in children. Polly's acting-out was far more severe and out of bounds of reality, but the patterns of rebellion, seductiveness, hostility, were the same. The worker's role with both these girls also remained the same: an understanding but firm and authoritative figure throughout.

Conclusion

Adolescents and schizophrenics are the outstanding exceptions to the rules of sharply focused casework therapy. In both these instances, the relationship of caseworker parent-surrogate takes precedence over the material discussed. Yet even here there is usually a succession of focuses, with perhaps more ramblings away from the focus in the case of schizophrenics. Despite the differences in their levels of ego development, there are similarities in their casework treatment.

The caseworker must often be prepared to be the emotional parent with all of the strains, privileges and responsibilities of authority, discipline, understanding and affection. The latter is especially important for schizophrenics, although adolescents, too, have extra sensitive antennae for the nonverbal emotional reactions of everyone around them. This, then, often makes it necessary for the caseworker also to assume responsibility as liaison between the client and his parents, interpreting each to the other. It is also important that the same caseworker take this responsibility seriously enough to be willing to stay with these patients as long as is necessary, whenever possible.

Chapter Nine

Other Exceptions

All rules are made to be broken. All clients are individuals. Each individual is unique. The technique of casework treatment must therefore be adapted to the "uniqueness" of the individual client. The only rule that cannot be broken is that in order to break a rule, the caseworker must have a reason or several reasons. This rationale must be based on a diagnostic clarification of the patient's patterns of functioning, how these affect the presenting symptoms, and how the breaking of a rule or even of all the rules will help this particular client reach the goal mutually agreed upon by client and worker.

Contrary to the thesis of this book, there are times when there is no focus that the client can be aware of. A client's neurotic conflicts may be so well-defended that any penetration would probably result in a psychotic illness. Yet this client is uncomfortable enough to seek help and obviously needs it. A 50-year-old man had been in analysis, individual psychotherapy and group psychotherapy with an analytically trained psychiatrist for some time. His male physician had felt that he could no longer work with him, but agreed that Mr. W.'s need to frustrate him as a man, his covert hostility, the strength of his defenses and the possibility of provoking a frank psychosis, made him inaccessible to any insightful therapy. He was therefore referred to a social agency with the recommendation that the caseworker be female. Psychological testing confirmed the clinical impressions of the referring psychiatrist. The plan evolved in the joint conference of social worker, supervisor and psychiatrist was to arrange cost-free weekly visits in which the caseworker would be approving and encouraging. No effort would be made to direct Mr. W. in any direction. He suffered from a severe obsessive neurosis in danger of decompensating. He was married to a very loving, accepting woman who was basically masochistic enough to tolerate Mr. W.'s sometimes quite irritating behavior. Mrs. W. who was seen twice, was of average intelligence, extremely impressed with her husband's brilliance, but unable to respond to any of his demands, except with the limited emotional responses Mr. W. sorely needed.

The worker was to represent the strong competent mother. Only the caseworker, as differentiated from Mr. W.'s real mother was to expect nothing from Mr. W. except what he realistically could and did achieve. As expected, Mr. W., a highly intellectualized and well-read man, complained often and loudly that his visits with the caseworker were accomplishing nothing. The caseworker must be incompetent. If he had not had such bad luck with his psychiatrist, he would terminate here, too. But this was his last chance. He had nowhere else to go. The worker consistently agreed that this was frustrating. When possible, she showed approval of his accomplishments. She sympathized openly with his failures and gave him great quantities of reassurance. This, too, is something we give rarely because reassurance in most instances seals off further exploration. Here, because Mr. W. was able to be somewhat dependent in a hostile fashion, and because he felt he was not investing any of his own meager financial resources in treatment, he continued on, talking about his theories of life, his strict principles of behavior, his troubles at work, his being a burden to his wife and anything that troubled him— which was usually everything. It was almost two years before Mr. W. began to show some improvement in his self-esteem and some lessening of his self-destructive, obsessive tendencies. He never achieved any deep meaningful insight, although he became aware of how angry he was at the world in general. At that time termination was indicated. Further work would have stirred up a hornet's nest of resistances. Analysis was indicated but not feasible. The focus here was entirely on the relationship. The verbal production varied and was wide-ranging. But the opportunity to talk about everything to an intelligent, understanding listener was extremely valuable.

Giving of advice, as distinct from making knowledge of resources available to clients, is usually a forbidden activity. If casework is aimed at helping people help themselves, advice-giving is apt to vitiate the process, make the client too dependent and the caseworker too authoritative. Yet there are times when advice is indicated and sometimes essential. The role of the caseworker as an authoritative parent with adolescents and schizophrenics has already been discussed. There are other times, too, when this role must be assumed. A parent in a panic state about the behavior of a child may well benefit from some direct counseling to relieve the immediate source of tension. This may be sufficient in itself or may be merely a means of making the parent accessible to more insightful treatment. Again, the diagnostic skill of the worker must be relied upon to make this differentiation. A parent confused by too much reading about how a parent should behave, might well benefit by some supportive counseling, frequently just enough to reinforce his own tendency to be more firm with a normally rebellious adolescent. A minimum of direct counseling frequently leaves such parents free to be more consistent and less dependent on books or magazine articles. Another parent, who is unconsciously provoking a child to hostile behavior, may get only temporary relief from counseling on a conscious level to be more firm and consistent with a frightened child. Following this superficial relief, the caseworker would have to decide who would need what kind of therapy, casework, individual or joint, referral to a psychiatric clinic, and so on.

A client arrived for his session in a state of shock. That morning he had found his brother dead of an overdose of barbiturates. After some relief from a tearful reliving of the finding of the body, the suicide note and the experiences with police and coroner's representatives, Mr. G. addressed himself to the problems still facing him. He had to tell his parents. His children were living in other cities. He was most fearful of the effect on his aged mother. There were also complications involved in the technicalities of the coroner's procedures and their effect on religious burial requirements, and in the legal implications of certain property which might be claimed, both by Mr. G. and his brother's estranged wife. The focus up to this point in treatment had been on Mr. G.'s need to be omnipotent and be responsible for and controlling of everyone close to him. The worker had recognized the unconscious needs for dependency to which this pattern was a reaction. The caseworker also recognized in this instance Mr. G.'s paralysis due, among other factors, to a conflict between Mr. G.'s dependency needs and his drive to take over and arrange everything. The latter course frightened him. He felt impelled to protect everyone but was uncertain as to how to go about it. The paralysis was the direct result of Mr. G.'s as yet unresolved therapeutic conflict. Immediate action was necessary. The burden of decision was too great for this particular individual at this particular point. The caseworker took over for him and, contrary to customary procedure, made a speech. Mr. G. was told to contact a close friend, who was a lawyer, to clarify the coroner's office procedures. He was to telephone his father to see him privately when Mr. G. with his wife's support could break the news to him. The decision of who should tell his mother and how she should be told, should be left to his father and his mother's physician. Then Mr. G. could feel free to share his mother's grief and comfort her. He was reminded of the support Mrs. G. had recently been able to give him because he had been more accepting of it, and was urged to avail himself of this further. He was also forewarned that in the normal grief of mourning, there was always an admixture of grief, relief and hostility, and not to be upset by whatever fantasies might be stimulated by this experience. Mr. G. reacted with visible decrease of tension. The interviews following this were preoccupied with more ventilation of feelings. But by that time, Mr. G. had somewhat integrated the experience and had faced the necessary pressing realities. He needed the comfort of the caseworker's strong support in order to do this. Having faced these reality pressures, he then had the strength and the distance to examine the distortions involved in his guilt, his hostility and his compassion—all related to his need to be omnipotent.

The list of exceptions can be endless. There are times when probably the most forbidden activities are soundly indicated. There must always be clarity on the part of the caseworker that the reasons for breaking the rules are based on the correct timing and understanding as to how this exception will further the self-development of the client and help him return to a period of more stable adjustment. Perhaps no rule is more rigidly observed than that which requires no physical contact between caseworker and client. The soundness of this rule cannot be questioned. Yet in a particular instance, an extremely ugly young woman was able to relax far more with her caseworker because once—and only once—that caseworker, sensing the great need for this reassurance, put her arm around the girl briefly as they walked down the hall. The worker had shown her understanding in a warm, knowledgeable fashion before this. But this young lady needed this particular kind of reassurance that she was not physically repulsive. Because both understood the meaning of this as well as the necessity for it, the gesture was not seductive, did not have to be repeated and did not have to be interpreted. It was an essential emotional experience.

There are even times when a caseworker may borrow a form of the tool of free association, again on a highly selective basis. A very silent woman might first gain support from the silence of the caseworker if given adequate preparation. Without this preparation, it would probably be felt as hostility. With understanding that this might well be the focus of treatment, or at least a first focus, this woman achieved sufficient comfort from the worker's obvious patience and nonverbal encouragement, finally to be enabled to talk of her fears about communicating with anyone lest she be ridiculed. The acceptance of herself as a silent person plus the acknowledgment that her thoughts about herself were important enough to warrant all the time necessary to wait for her production, made it possible for her to share her thoughts with another human being for the first time.

This adaptation of the technique of free association usually is remarkably productive. Like in the dreams presented to caseworkers, the unconscious of the client is highly selective and discriminating in choosing what it will uncover, and sometimes has a better sense of the appropriateness of what it shall uncover than either the client or the worker. Hence the need and responsibility of the worker to listen so carefully.

Finally, from time to time an application is received for casework treatment, usually by a family agency, psychiatric clinic or private practitioner, from a client who quickly demonstrates such depth of insight and such accessibility to his own preconscious or unconscious motivation, that the skilled caseworker is quickly trapped into more intensive therapy than is usual. These are the individuals whose casework treatment would be difficult to distinguish from psychoanalytic treatment. These are the records too frequently not exhibited as examples of a type of casework practice that is fairly common but looked upon with serious question by a segment of the social work profession. Here, too, the focus is important and limits the extent of the exploration, but the depth of the treatment is determined by the client. These clients may have the same accessibility to their unconscious as frequently is considered characteristic of schizophrenics. But there is no question that these individuals are neither psychotic nor predisposed to psychosis. They are usually of high intelligence and function well and effectively in reality despite a segment of the personality which is disturbed and troublesome.

Mrs. Y. was referred to a child guidance clinic because she and her 12-year-old son were constantly embattled —at times to the point of literally beating each other up. Mrs. Y. intitially gave a history of her son, Richard, having been a hyperactive child from birth. He had been a constant source of irritation to her since he was the third of six children born in quick succession in the first eight years of her marriage. She felt guilty about her obvious rejection of Richie and was now fearful that she may have "permanently damaged him." His outbursts of temper were so excessive.

Psychological testing and psychiatric evaluation determined that Richie's chief difficulty was his jealousy of his siblings and his need for proof of love from his mother. In staff conference, Mrs. Y. was assigned to a caseworker after the psychiatrist gave her this report. Mrs. Y. was eager to resolve her guilt and hostility to Richie, and regular interviews were scheduled. Mrs. Y. gave a personal history of growing up in a large family where she felt neglected by both her parents. She was the "good" girl who became closest to her mother by helping more than any of her siblings with the housework. Her father was tyrannical and frightening. She avoided him as much as possible. One sister and one brother were especially rebellious, and father was constantly berating them and often beat them. This terrified Mrs. Y. into further obedience and withdrawal within herself. She was very bright and quick in school, always fearful, however, of displeasing her teachers. She was very attractive, and in her teens had many dates. But aggressive, attractive men frightened her, and she rarely dated the same man more than once. She married a bright, emotionally withdrawn man with whom she had to be the aggressor both in courtship and in proposing marriage.

In the process of taking the history, it became clear to both the caseworker and Mrs. Y. that her problem lay in her fear of aggressive men. This seemed obviously fairly simple to relate to her fear of her father. Her choice of her husband reassured her against these fears. Her hyperactive son reawakened them. Within ten interviews, her relationship with Richie began to improve and termination in the not-too-distant future began to be considered by the caseworker. It had not yet been discussed with Mrs. Y. In the eleventh session, Mrs. Y. began to question the basis of her fears of her father and quite quickly produced her hostile fantasies of emasculating men and trapping them in her power. It also became clear that she had been far more fearful of her mother than of her father. In the milieu of a benign relationship with a female caseworker, Mrs. Y. was able to bring forth her hitherto repressed fantasies. An additional staff conference reassured the worker sufficiently to enable her to continue working with Mrs. Y. for two years until these fantasies were resolved. Mrs. Y. eventually recognized in retrospect the sexual implication of her relationship with Richie and was able to be of great help to him during his early adolescent tentative heterosexual relationships. Her acceptance of her husband became less fraught with ambivalence, and her social relationships with men became more comfortable.

Conclusion

All rules are made to be broken. Any unorthodox form of casework treatment is valid if the course of treatment is clearly related to the needs and capacities of the client. If any situation can be said to demand more concentrated diagnostic thinking, the times when exceptional modes of casework treatment are to be used, would be predominant. The limitations of the caseworker's skills and administrative policy are additional factors in determining exceptions. But even the rules of the agency may be stretched, on occasion, if the rationale is sound.

This is a necessarily brief chapter. The exceptions to

the rules are necessarily few—else we return to aimless meandering. But it is vitally important to stress flexibility in dealing with human beings.

Chapter Ten

Private Practice

As social work progressed from providing essential services to understanding and exploring services to human beings, its coverage to more and more socioeconomic levels became broader. It is a trite statement, but it needs repetition. If social work has something valuable to offer individuals, families, and groups, then it would be gross discrimination on the part of the profession to limit its help to lower income groups. Many agencies salve their consciences by setting up a sliding scale of fees. It has happened that millionaires have consulted agencies and paid the maximum fee, which has been disporportionately low. We must seriously question whether these people are really paying their bills in full. Does a philanthropically supported agency, set up to serve a community, have the right to withhold its services or not to charge those who can afford a fee more proportionate to the real ability of the client to pay and more commensurate with the real cost of that service to the agency? Does an agency set up by fund raising groups to help people who cannot afford to pay for services, have the right to siphon off its valuable time and personnel to provide service to those who can afford to pay for service elsewhere? An agency with a waiting list has the responsibility to carry out the function set for it by the community that pays the bills.

Much more important is the factor of public relations. A profession that says, "No one can use our services who can afford to pay for them," is really saying, "Our services are not worth very much." Only as the community at large pays for social work services which are or become valuable to the individuals in the community, will these same people be willing to pay well to provide these services for others. Social workers' salaries and status fall far below those of other professions with equal standards. It is the conviction of this author that the establishment of professional acceptance of private practice is an important and essential step towards erasing this inequality.

It was with great pleasure that I read a quotation from Mary Richmond's *What is Social Case Work,* written in 1922, in which she predicts the establishment of private practice.

> "How rapidly social casework will develop a private practice of its own cannot be predicted, but it should be evident from the examples given in this book that the skill here described can be utilized quite as well in the homes of the rich, as in those of the poor, that, in the one as in the other, personality can be thwarted and retarded, developed and enriched."*

Private practice is often regarded as one level of a continuum that begins with public welfare at the other end.

*Quoted in Editorial Notes of *Journal of Social Case Work,* Vol. *XXX,* 1959, p 563.

This is unfortunately necessarily so. Practice without supervision requires highly trained, skilled practitioners. As long as public welfare remains a paper-pushing, investigative and social referral agency, the skills required are less. This will be discussed in greater detail in the following chapter. For the present I would like to offer some of my own experiences. Because I have been somewhat of a pioneer in this field, I shall attempt to set down some of the occupational delights and hazards of the private practice of casework. This must necessarily be a personal record in great part.

It was not until I had been in social work for more than fifteen years that I felt prepared to enter private practice. This was partially because so much of my early experience was in public agencies but also because I did not feel that the training in school was adequate. It was not until I had had six years of good, well-supervised clinical experience that I felt certain that I knew what I was doing and could do it without the support of constant supervision. I should add that in my last year or two at a clinic, I had worked without supervision. Consultation, of course, was available when necessary. I should also add that I was then completing my personal analysis, something I feel is also essential for the independent practitioner.

Then I felt ready and I did it. I started on a halftime basis. My position in the community at that time was most fortunate, since I had then worked in the two most important clinics in Los Angeles and had had the opportunity of working with almost all the members of what was then a comparatively small group of psychoanalysts and psychoanalytically oriented psychiatrists, and psychiatric social workers.

At first I received my major support primarily from the psychiatrists. Social workers were horrified. They remained personally friendly and were most cooperative when I requested service for one of my patients or the relative of a patient. But in the first few years, I received no referrals from social workers. And one prominent social worker, who has now confessed the error of her ways, once publicly denounced me as a traitor to my profession. I am sure if there were an identifying badge or epaulets, she would have ripped them off with delight. That was in 1950.

During the past decade, this attitude has gradually changed. Referrals from social workers have increased. Interestingly enough, the majority of referrals are of relatives and friends of individual social workers rather than of agency applicants. At first, the question was raised as to whether independent practice really was social work. How could a social worker be a social worker outside of a social agency? Then it changed to grudging recognition. Social work may not need the support of agency structure, but there is too much that is undefined in our field, so how can we identify this newest area of practice? Then we progressed to recognition of our existence, and the fact that something should be done about it, but too many other things have to be done first. Then we had a national committee working very hard to set up standards for social workers in private practice. The delegate assembly had approved minimum standards, and the national board of directors had authorized the study of further steps necessary. Our war-weary combatants now have time to rest and heal their wounds. We feel as if we have been accepted back into the fold and we are proud and grateful that we no longer have to fight our own profession.

The mechanical process of setting up an office is comparatively simple: a pleasant office, a desk, two chairs and a telephone—plus the essential telephone answering service. Many social workers rent time in the offices of other therapists, usually making a separate arrangement with a telephone exchange. It is essential that current, past and future patients have a central place where the worker may be reached.

It usually takes three to five years to build up a practice to the point where the social worker can estimate an average annual income. Most initial referrals are made on the basis of personal professional relationships. After that time, referrals begin to come from patients themselves. No one to my knowledge has been able to gauge the flow of referrals. One of the most difficult adjustments the independent practitioner has to make is to the periods of feast and famine. This, of course, means that we have to adjust to an uncertain and irregular income. After years of earning a specific salary, this is quite difficult. Difficult, too, is the anxiety of where the next referral is going to come from? Almost everyone who chooses to be in private practice full time has faced moments of feeling that in a month when so-and-so terminates, and so-and-so leaves town, he is going to have an almost empty schedule. What will he do then? Somehow, manna always falls from heaven and the appointment book fills up again. And over the years, we become accustomed to this. A keen and alert awareness of this anxiety is essential for the worker to avoid the temptation to seduce the client, albeit unconsciously, into continuing in treatment beyond the essential goals determined at intake. The self-discipline of focused treatment is an invaluable asset at this point.

My fee schedule varies depending on the income and responsibilities of the individual. I do no great financial exploration. In the first hour, I discuss fees, telling the patient what my scale is. I point out that this is an ongoing financial responsibility the patient is undertaking and that we both have to be realistic and honest about this. It has been my experience that no patient to date has requested too low a fee. Occasionally someone agrees to a higher fee than he can truly afford, and an adjustment must be made later. This has been rare. If the income of a low-rate patient increases, his fee is increased. This too he is prepared for in the initial interview so that only infrequently is there need for much further discussion when the fee is raised. Almost always this can be related to the patient's dynamics and is of therapeutic value.

For myself, the greatest advantage of private practice is freedom. If I have cancellations or several free hours, I can do as I please, unhampered by administrative restrictions. Reports, dictation, conferences—all the addenda which take up so much time in an agency or clinic—are eliminated. Almost all one's working time is spent seeing patients. And then we are free. This, too, is an area where private practice can be a demonstration for agencies. I do keep records on each individual I see. As an exponent of terse diagnostic recording, and since my records are for myself alone, an hour with a patient may be recorded in one or two sentences. The initial sessions are, of course, far more detailed. I find that the ten minutes or so between patients are quite adequate for the kinds of records I find necessary. Some social workers in private practice keep ongoing records; some keep them in great detail, taking notes during the interview. This, of course, is a matter of individual choice. For myself, I find I cannot listen alertly if I take notes—so I do not.

Another satisfaction I find in private practice is the role of public relations representative for the field of social work. Patients frequently ask what I am and what my training is. Most are surprised to find that I am neither a psychologist or psychiatrist. I explain that I am a graduate of a school of social work with many years of experience in agencies and clinics. I also tell them that while their surprise is natural, since until recently so few social workers were engaged in private practice, the service they are about to receive is no different from that offered by social workers in many agencies and clinics.

The primary disadvantage of private practice is the loneliness and isolation that almost all of us feel. Most of us have tried to continue our work within N.A.S.W. Another major disadvantage is the difficulty of finding opportunities to teach what we know. Many of us have enjoyed training workers and students. Rarely does anyone in full time private practice have this opportunity. Some of us have resolved this by allocating some of our time to consultation. This is an area that, I believe, the field in general is overlooking to a great extent. The social workers in private practice represent a tremendous storehouse of experience and training. I do not think sufficient use is made of this. More agencies should call upon us and utilize what we can offer. Some are beginning to do so, to the benefit of all concerned.

The other aspect of loneliness is the loss of frequent contact with colleagues. It is not so much the formal staff conferences that are missed. These are always available in some form. More important is the informal interchange that occurs when you meet a colleague in the hall or drop into his office to work off your own accumulated questions and emotions about a particular interview. My office is in a section I refer to as the "medical ghetto," since so many medical buildings are congregated there: the famous Beverly Hills. It is almost impossible to go out on the street and not meet someone you know. But, although everyone—regardless of discipline—complains about this kind of isolation, the street and the lunch rooms are not conducive to ventilation and catharsis.

Relief is focused in more social and personal communication.

True, every social worker in private practice that I know has consultation available. Many make arrangements to see a psychoanalyst on a regular or irregular basis. This, of course, is not the same as the support one feels from one's colleagues. But it is valuable and essential nonetheless. But here once again, I am going to stick my neck out and wait to have it chopped off. As one analyst once told me, "How can I cure your paranoia, when it's based on reality?" I feel strongly that if a social worker needs to have regular consultation weekly so that someone else has to direct his activity with all or almost all of his patients, he is not ready for private practice. As I have stated earlier, a social worker should not engage in private practice until and unless he is working independently in a clinic or agency and has demonstrated that he knows how and when to request consultation. I also feel that as we continue to practice independently, we seek consultation less and less frequently. If we cannot grow and develop and become truly independent, we should not be in private practice. This is not to say that we never need or seek consultation. But we must become secure and confident of our judgment and demonstrate that we are educable and have learned. For myself, I may find that for six or eight months, or even a year, I may need no consultation, and then find that within a period of a few weeks or months, I have had quite a number of consultations. Just as in social agencies, consultations with colleagues of any of the therapeutic disciplines, and with lawyers and financial advisers, are utilized freely as indicated. I also believe that social workers beginning in private practice should use more experienced private practitioners as consultants as well as psychiatrists and psychoanalysts. I have served as consultant to psychologists and occasionally with social workers. Recently, I had the fascinating experience of supervising a lawyer who was doing what he called prelegal counseling, but which turned out to be an amalgam of legal counseling based on knowledge of law and human behavior, a rarity these days, and good old-fashioned casework. This lawyer is now planning to enroll in a school of social work. We in private practice are free to be available for all kinds of odd jobs if only we would be called upon more often.

Who are my patients? Since I have had little experience with children, I see only adults. Since I am particularly interested in older adolescents and ambulatory schizophrenics, these always are represented in my list of patients. Patients come with the usual problems represented in the intake of any family agency: "My husband is leaving me and I don't know how to face the divorce and living alone." "I can't control my son or daughter's rebelliousness. Will you help her or him?" "I cannot be a good mother to my children. I feel sometimes as though I'd like to hurt them. Yet I love them and want to be a good mother." "I don't know how to make friends. I'm lonely and not doing as well on my job as I should because I don't know how to get along with people." Occasionally a patient will say, "Dr. X. says I should come to you. All I know is that I have this ache and pain, and Dr. X. says there's nothing wrong with me. I trust Dr. X., and here I am." Some people need a great deal of help in understanding that they have an emotional problem. Some come with considerable insight and awareness.

The economic status of my clientele varies from lower middle-class, for whom therapy is a considerable sacrifice, to those for whom even my highest fee is no burden whatsoever. Some have had unhappy experiences with clinics. Some do not feel they can wait their turn on a long waiting list. Some prefer a nonmedical therapist because the term psychiatrist or psychoanalyst is too frightening. This is especially true of schizoid and borderline schizophrenics. I never, under any circumstances, accept individuals who can be diagnosed as depressive or actively psychotic because I feel these should be treated only by physicians. No matter how good our training and how skilled we may be as diagnosticians, we still do not have the particular medical training which enables the physician to be more alert to danger signals pointing to the need for medication or hospitalization. If a patient is mildly depressed and I think there is possibly no danger of its intensification, I insist that the patient be seen by a psychiatrist. I tell the patient quite frankly that as a nonmedical practitioner, I cannot accept responsibility for his treatment without medical consultation. Except in one situation where the individual did not return after the first interview, there has been no difficulty about this.

It is also equally important that social workers be overly cautious where physical symptoms are presented. In this heyday of psychosomatic medicine, too many people, including some physicians, are emphasizing the psyche to the neglect of the soma. Patients are frequently the first to discredit some pain with an offhand comment, "Oh, I know this is psychosomatic." My answer is always, "Yes, it is possible. However, no one but your physician an determine this." If a physical symptom persists and the patient does not initiate a visit to his doctor, I will initiate discussion of this and try to work through the resistance. I am not implying that our patients have to run to their doctors at any sign of physical discomfort. It is not necessary for individuals to become hypochondriacs to ensure our feelings of security. But I do think we can learn to be cautious.

Patients are seen once or twice a week, rarely three

times a week, the frequency depending on the patient's needs. Many are seen on a supportive basis, such as a schizoid young woman who is functioning but who would be totally unable to tolerate any insight deeper than that her tie to her mother so infantilized her that she had difficulty in being on her own after her mother's death. This much insight took several years to develop. This client was seen only once weekly and was given much counseling about where she might go to meet people, etc. Others readily develop considerable insight working with preconscious material and unconscious derivatives. A client may talk about being jealous of a sister who was father's favorite, avoid the oedipal implications of this, and yet gain considerable ego strength and insight from this situation. Occasionally a client sails right in and is quite comfortable with recognizing previously unconscious drives and feelings. But here we get into the differences between casework, psychotherapy and psychoanalysis. Occasionally, and only occasionally, there are none.

In summary, the ego strength of the client determines the type of treatment. If a client comes to me with a long-standing chronic character disorder, I invariably refer him to a psychoanalyst. In general, then, I would say that my clients are individuals with acute disturbances which can be helped with some characterological change but not necessitating the complete overhaul represented by psychoanalysis.

I refer clients for psychological testing on a selective basis—sometimes at the beginning of treatment, sometimes after some period of treatment—when I feel I would like to know more about the underlying dynamics of a particular problem than the patient is able to reveal. I may also ask for psychological testing in preparation for consultation in order to give the consultant more information than I feel I have available in the material produced by the client. Again, this is discussed frankly with the client. The cost to the client and the potential value or lack of value are discussed in as much detail as seems indicated. The type of tests and similar questions are also described.

Private practice can and will do much to raise the profession in public esteem. The effect of increased remuneration on social work salaries is inevitable. The streamlining of practice, which enables social workers to devote more time to practice and less to peripheral activity, is another area that can eventually make its influence felt in social work practice. Above all, the willingness of the profession to be proud of its maturity, which says workers eventually grow up to function as truly independent practitioners, marks a great advance.

The caseloads of the private practitioner vary not at all from those of a generic family agency. The major difference is that the caseworker in private practice is freer to be discriminating in the kind of client he chooses to accept for treatment. The self-awareness of the caseworker in private practice must be highly developed. He should know what his particular skills are and what his weaknesses are. He will refer elsewhere those applicants for his service to whom he feels he cannot be particularly helpful because of his own personal preferences and prejudices, or because of the lack of a particular kind of experience. The rejection, however, must be ego-syntonic and free of hostility to the applicant.

Mrs. J. came for help with her mentally retarded child. Mrs. J. herself was of slightly less than average intelligence, slow of speech and of thought. The worker found herself impatient in the very first interview. He advised Mrs. J. that her problem required a special knowledge of certain kinds of resources which were not readily available to him. Another caseworker with experience in this field could be more helpful. A referral was made. No fee was charged for this interview, which was very brief.

Karen A. came for help with her marriage. She had had an affair with her employer which had recently terminated. Karen could not leave her husband because she was fearful of the effect of divorce on her 12-year-old daughter. Karen was a chronic depressive, masochistic character who was married to a hostile, passive, suspicious man. Her lover had been dependent on her but had known how to enjoy many things. John, her husband, was even more dependent. He would do anything she requested. But he never seemed to be interested in anything. He was a silent, unfriendly escort. There was practically no real communication between them. The sense of power, the gratifications Karen obviously achieved in this marriage in which she relished the role of martyr, were noted but not questioned. The focus of treatment was her hostility which she did not recognize completely. After ten interviews, John was persuaded to participate in one of Karen's sessions. He came reluctantly but did so because he "wanted to do everything and anything that would help Karen. He was aware that she was becoming somewhat depressed." Having been fortified by previous sessions, Karen took the initiative to ask whether John did not think he might have something to do with her depression. John looked amazed and then very dramatically burst out with an explosive statement of how angry Karen made him with her constant demands. It was Karen's turn to be amazed. She burst into tears. John shrugged his shoulders and commented that that was why he never resisted her demands or tried to express his feelings about anything. Karen replied that she was crying only because this was the first time John had ever indicated his anger. She wept for all the years John had isolated himself out of fear of Karen. This was too much power. She did not want it. Mr. A. refused to return for further joint sessions. He was fearful of further such explosions. Mrs. A. continued to come for a weekly session for the next three months. Following the joint session, communication and rapport between Mr. and Mrs. A. had begun to build slowly but consistently. Mrs. A. was unconsciously pleased to be able to take the major share of the responsibility for this change by continuing in treatment alone. But she was able to respect her husband and his feelings more and more.

Mrs. Joanna R. came for help because she was in a process of divorcing her husband. He was too quarrelsome and made the home impossible for Mrs. R. and the children. A great deal of money was involved. Business interests had to be separated, and Mr. R. was fighting for the custody of the children. Mrs. R., a borderline schizophrenic who had been treated for transitory psychotic episodes previously, was seen for the year it took to get all of these details settled. There were frequent conferences with the lawyers to evaluate how much of Mrs. R.'s reactions were based on reality. There were referrals to group work facilities for the children, vocational counseling for Mrs. R. who needed work for its ego supportive function, and conferences with the psychiatrist who had treated Mrs. R. previously and was still seeing her at long intervals to control her medication.

Then there are the clients like the adolescent and ambulatory schizophrenic described in a previous chapter who require and receive intensive and lengthy casework treatment.

Conclusion

Private practice is now an accepted area of casework. It is beginning to be extended to group work, community organization and possibly research. It is the same practice. Whether in an agency, or in a clinic, or in his own office, the caseworker is responsible for upholding the tradition, skill, knowledge and discipline of his profession. Hopefully, the higher income of social workers in private practice and the use of social work services by higher income groups will improve the status of the profession as a whole in the community at large. Equally important is the greater availability of social work services to higher income groups who can afford to pay for these services. This leaves the agencies freer to spend the money contributed by the community for philanthropic purposes more exclusively for those who truly cannot afford them.

Chapter Eleven

Public Assistance

It is traditional in the social work profession to think of public assistance as being at the opposite end of the therapeutic spectrum from private practice. This is true only in a limited sense. The skilled practitioner in both of these fields is concerned with people's emotional problems. It is true that public assistance agencies are primarily concerned with providing relief from financial pressures, while the caseworker in private practice is primarily concerned with helping individuals secure relief from internal pressures. We have seen, however, that in private practice the caseworker is presented with individuals subject to many external pressures. Now more than ever, the profession of social work and public welfare authorities are recognizing that in many instances the public welfare clients need help with their emotional problems if they are ever to be free of the need for public assistance. Perhaps the field of social work will have to give up its claim to be the profession that gives all kinds of help to everyone in need of it. This will leave the practitioner in the field of public welfare freer to use his energies and skills to help those who need them most. Those people who need financial assistance alone could well be referred to a branch of the agency set up in a manner similar to that of unemployment insurance. Those who are likely to become the multiproblem or chronically dependent families without some intensive casework assistance would then be the concern of the caseworkers. Each agency could then decide for itself in cooperation with local schools of social work on the value of an in-service training program or possibly a one-year certificate curriculum to prepare potential workers to help the so-called normal families or to spot those needing referral for more intensive casework treatment. The intake department would necessarily need the workers with more training and experience. The investigating and "financial giving" department might possibly be trained in the knowledge and use of community resources. But the more the profession restricts its activity, the better can it husband its acknowledgedly meager resources. The more the profession concentrates on the areas of greatest need, the greater will be the benefit to the community in terms of reduced welfare costs and, even more important, the return to the community of those individuals who can become contributing members to their communities.

There are numerous complaints that an insufficient number of graduates of schools of social work enter the field of public welfare. There is certainly a great awareness of the need for the skills trained social workers can offer. Now that there is more awareness of this, a delegation of the burdensome tasks, which are burdensome precisely because they call upon skills which are not the province of the trained social worker, would do much to increase the attractiveness of public welfare services to social work graduates. With this kind of clarification, it will be far easier to support the claim for higher salaries comparable to those set for private agencies and therefore easier to recruit skilled practitioners.

A worker with a large caseload, even with excellent training, can do little more than call on a family briefly once a month, if that often, try to make the most obviously necessary referrals (such as to clinics, legal agencies, employment bureaus), ask the customary routine questions, check on any possibilities of income and leave. It is this emphasis on the social worker as an investigator that has contributed so much to the distasteful public image of the social worker as well as to the distaste of the social worker for the public welfare job.

The following is a typical entry of a public welfare worker genuinely interested in helping this family, but working so hard at it that nothing could be gained except more hostility.

May, 1958: Worker made home visit. The shades were down and the household dark and dreary. Mr. Benedict had had a severe heart attack during the night. Mrs. Benedict became hysterical, hostile and accusatory. She accused her social worker of checking up on her and prying into all aspects of her private life. She screamed that she wished to discontinue the Aid to Needy Children Program and that she wanted no part of the agency or of the worker. She was so violent in her accusations that the worker became extremely concerned and called the family physician, Dr. Cohen. He agreed that Mrs. Benedict had had all that she could handle and wrote a letter requesting a housekeeper for one month in order to take some pressure off her. A housekeeper was arranged for and worker called Mrs. Benedict to find out how she was. Mrs. Benedict became furious and accused the social worker of spreading the word around town that she was crazy. She said she knew the social worker called the public health nurse and Dr. Cohen. The situation was so bad it did not seem recoverable, and the case was transferred to a new worker. The worker who had come to an impasse with Mrs. Benedict left a short summary. School reports had been received. Tom was doing well in his grades and all the other children were accomplishing; none had problems at school. Before the blow-up worker reported that she had talked at one time to Mr. Benedict who had told her that his wife no longer loved him. Mrs. Benedict had also said that her husband no longer loved her. Both said that they are very concerned about their children and will stay together for this reason. Mrs. Benedict said that she was not the kind to run out on a sick man. However, Mr. Benedict has started to accuse her of having boyfriends and becomes very upset whenever she leaves the house. He accuses her in front of the children and this causes her much anguish. At one point the worker had referred her back to the Family Service Agency. Worker had also made plans for her to go to the Salvation Army Mother and Children's Camp for a rest.

Unfortunately, workers in public agencies, especially, because of their insufficient training, try to do too much too quickly. They preempt to themselves, albeit unconsciously, the role of omnipotent gods and try too hard to "do" for people instead of being able to understand these people as individuals with their own strengths and defenses. Even people receiving public assistance have a right to make decisions for themselves. This is too often forgotten and overlooked.

Parallel to this attitude and reinforcing and supporting it to some extent, is the question of the authority
which the law vests in the social workers it hires as its
representatives. There are some situations that are difficult for the individuals concerned and that have to be
presented realistically. Action on these without respect
for the client's feelings makes further help to these clients impossible unless the barrier or resentment can be
eradicated first. Thus in the record noted above the following entries are found:

> *April, 1957:* A joint visit by both county and
> state workers was paid. Mrs. Benedict informed
> the worker that she had been home to Texas for
> fourteen days, she was so tired and nervous that
> she needed to get away. Her half-brother had
> sent her fare to come and rest up. The family
> had found a way to keep Tom's insurance pol-
> icy. They have only three more payments on
> their car; their TV and automatic washer are
> paid for. The doctor ordered a private phone so
> there would be no delay in reaching a physi-
> cian. Mrs. Benedict reported her husband had
> had another heart attack and been hospitalized
> for several days.
> *May, 1957:* Hold placed on the June warrant for
> excess personal property. Family not eligible
> for assistance. June warrant canceled.

No attempt was made to prepare Mr. and Mrs. B. for
this or to explain its necessity. At no time was either Mr.
or Mrs. B. given the opportunity to express their feelings
about this reality, so that it is no surprise that Mrs. B. has
so much hostility to her worker. It can easily be explained that the worker had insufficient time to handle
this properly. To the worker, this was part of the rou-

tine. To the B. family, it was just another serious deprivation which also was damaging to their self-respect.

The role of any social worker in an authoritarian setting is always a complicated and difficult one. He represents what frequently appears to his client as an extremely harsh reality. It is only through mutual recognition of the client's right to deem this harsh reality, that, as in any casework situation, the client can learn to come to terms with his reality. This perhaps frequently needs to be a first focus of the relationship between the public assistance worker and his client. Public assistance is rarely adequate, and the many rules and regulations are often confusing and are first preceived by clients solely as sources of irritation and frustration. Respect for these feelings and the understanding of their nature will be rewarding to the worker and the agency in the clues they provide to the underlying needs and behavioral patterns of the recipients. Diagnostically, they are of inestimable value in hypothesizing the strengths and dependency needs of the family. At times, the expression of anger may be healthy; at others, the type of expression may, as in the case of Mrs. Benedict, indicate an inability to face one more pressure. These reactions are helpful in enabling the trained worker to determine whether this family or individual needs help other than financial in order to maintain its independence and to work towards the goal of terminating public assistance. The way in which a family or individual goes about accepting the limitations of public assistance tells us much about their capabilities in coping with other realities.

The family whose negative experience was quoted above, was eventually chosen for a special family project for intensive casework oriented to the rehabilitation of the family as a unit. In her first interview with the trained worker, Mrs. B. had an opportunity to ventilate some of her feelings about her past experience with the agency. It is quite obvious that she has the worker's respect and that the worker is thinking of Mrs. B. and her family first and the public welfare regulations second.

> *Intake Appointment:* Mrs. Benedict came in one hour late for her appointment. She had taken Tom to the clinic for an appointment. Mrs. Benedict is 35 years old. She is an attractive, intelligent, highly articulate person. She seemed depressed, but one recognized she had been a vigorous person at some point; and she still seemed to have a sense of self-respect and dignity. She related well and seemed to trust me fairly soon in the interview; we were able to explore some of her past problems with the public welfare agency. She was very bitter and as she talked about selling the car and her insurance and other properties, she shuddered visibly; she became rather hysterical as she recounted this experience. She feels this action was not necessary. She commented that thank goodness she had had one or two social workers who were all right; otherwise she would think that they were all right; otherwise she would think that they were all "horrible, mean, terrible people." It is quite possible that the social workers who were "all right" had no realistic need to present deprivation to the family.
>   She told me that her husband is twenty years older than she, and that since his illness he does not want her to go to church, and she has stopped this. He wants her at home with him and the children, and he always feels his heart and gets upset if she does insist on leaving to take care of things or because she must get away

in order to get a little time to herself and to think things out. She told me that she had seen a worker at the Family Service Agency for a few months who had helped her to express herself, but she said her husband was not able to talk about anything or talk about his illness and she feels this is very hard on him. She said that she just wished she could get away, that she cannot stand being so held in. She is worried that he will die and that she does not want to do anything wrong; she feels if something happened to him she could not live with the guilt she would feel. She said that on many occasions in a panic she has rushed him to the hospital in a taxi and tests have indicated that it was not a real heart attack. This upsets her very much because she never knows when he is really having a heart attack or just having a "mock attack," as she called it. She said that she wished her husband could accept the inevitable, that what one can't help one must accept, but he is unable to do this. She thinks perhaps she has been unable to do so too.

Without mutual respect, the referral to community resources is usually interpreted as part of the authoritarian commands which must be resisted. More and more, the special projects set up to help families who have been longtime recipients of public assistance are discovering that the first resistance is to a positive relationship with a caseworker. The first focus has to be on "working through" the many years of accumulated mistrust and essential defiance of what has seemed to many clients to be unnecessarily disrespectful authoritative behavior. To some clients, the authoritarian attitude is an answer to their neurotic needs. Some can only meet authoritarianism with greater deterioration. When this manner of the social worker is used ubiquitously, without discrimination, it is always hostile and destructive.

In public assistance there is necessarily more emphasis on helping families meet their reality problems. After all, they were motivated to become clients primarily because of external pressures. It is a truism that a hungry man is not interested in ideas about anything—even his own emotional problems. A family beset with budgetary problems is in the same position. The most eager worker willing to be helpful cannot tell any family how to budget their money without running the risk of depreciating the right of that family to self-determination and self-respect. The worker is most helpful when he can offer himself as a resource consultant to the family to be used for their benefit. This is in direct contrast to "advising;" telling a family how their money should be spent.

A truism frequently overlooked is the fact that in each of us is a drive towards health, stability and self-realization. Nothing is more antithetical to this than to have to channel the energies of a family into the necessity of fighting the public assistance worker in order to stay alive. Again the basic social work concept must be remembered: "Accept the client where he is."

> During May and June the interviews focused primarily on the difficult marital situation and the parents' relationship to their children. Mr. Benedict's illness had put an end to their high hopes that their children would have college educations and 'dignified jobs.' We discussed scholarships, part-time college jobs and other possibilities for the children, even with the low family income.
>
> There were so many financial and physical crises that most of my time was spent dealing with them. It seemed impossible to find a short,

even sequence of interviews to concentrate on the Benedicts' marital problems.

One of the most valuable services I provided to this family, services which in turn seemed to make it much easier for them to trust me and to relate to me, were things that I provided through special needs. In addition, they always had papers and letters from various organizations, agencies, lawyers and courts ready when I arrived; they asked me to interpret to them. In that setting with this family the letters sounded like gibberish and on several occasions I had to call a lawyer for consultation about the meaning of specific dispatches—from the district attorney's office, for example, about debts the family had owed at the time of Mr. Benedict's heart attack, and about certain matters pertaining to the OAIS. The agency letters were often in "graduate division language."

This family was seen for little more than six months. Many problems were recognized but were left untouched. The skilled worker equally recognized that the two most important areas that had to be chosen for intensive work with this family were: (1) the reestablishment of the family's self-respect through a mutually respectful relationship between the worker and the family; (2) the use of the worker as a liaison between this family and the community, so that the family would be enabled to use these services for their own benefit. By the time the worker had to leave this family, both goals had been accomplished. A previous referral to the Family Service Agency had been a failure. Now the Benedict family seemed ready to accept such a referral. They understood the internal pressures which motivated such a referral and were ready to work on these problems. Above all, they had hope for themselves based on their recognition of reality limitations and reality possibilities.

The Benedict family applied for public assistance because of Mr. Benedict's serious illness. With the enforced dependency, Mr. Benedict became suspicious of Mrs. Benedict and resentful of her greater capacity to manage the family affairs. Because Mrs. Benedict was the primary person in the family who conducted the business with the public welfare authorities, Mr. Benedict's role in the family became less and less important. As his effectiveness decreased, his suspicions increased. The trained worker recognized this but made no effort to treat it directly. He did make every effort possible to include Mr. Benedict in the family planning and in various ways made it very clear that he was reinforcing Mr. Benedict's role as head of the household rather than pre-empting that role. The worker was also diagnostically determining that the deeper, more basic issues between Mr. and Mrs. Benedict could not be resolved in this limited time available. He therefore utilized his recognition to keep uninvolved in a situation in which he could not be helpful. Instead, he referred the couple to a family agency when the Benedicts had been adequately prepared for accepting such help.

Here again we have a form of family therapy that is as old as casework itself. The disturbances within the family were accurately diagnosed. The way in which this particular public agency could be helpful determined the focus of casework treatment. What could not be treated within the framework of this agency was not stirred up unnecessarily. But even more important is the knowledge that even if Mr. and Mrs. Benedict could not have been referred to a family agency, they and their family were in far better relationship to themselves and each other by the end of this worker's contact with them.

In all of the history of western civilization, the poor have been identified as liars and cheats. This springs from a partial truth. Not every person bred in poverty is a liar and a cheat. Most are not. But for many, cunning has often had to substitute for employment. Resourcefulness replaced resources. Curiously, there is a direct relationship between ego strength and "antisocial" behavior. The more passive and accepting of poverty and public welfare an individual is, the less is the likelihood of his "cheating." The more eager a welfare recipient is to tell everyone about his standard of living, the more necessary does the "cheating" become.

The ghetto culture varies with each particular ghetto. But perhaps common to all is the general acceptance of welfare as a way of life and the need to outsmart the social worker. Rules and regulations have been made to outsmart ghetto residents. Battle lines were drawn many years ago. It is not until the social workers and their administrators can comprehend that lying and cheating often represent healthy adaptations to unhealthy, despair-ridden situations that the impasse will be broken. The answers are complex. But so are our systems of helping. Families have been known to be accountable to numerous agencies, each represented by a social worker who may be a different person on each visit. How can any meaningful relationship be built on that?

At the moment, it would be difficult to merge all agencies into one. There are the vested interests of administrators of programs to be guarded. There is too much emphasis on specialization even in the field of social welfare. Steps are being taken here and there to break down these barriers. In the meantime, informal agreements amongst concerned social workers can lead the way to "One Family, One Social Worker." One agency representative can be the bearer of rehabilitation while the others serve as resource consultants.

Conclusion

The legal restrictions of public assistance may limit the extent and depth of treatment the caseworker may be able to give to a client. The skillful use of diagnostic evaluation of the needs of a family which can be met, within those limits will enhance the effectiveness and ultimately the economical administration of any public welfare program. The cautious use of the authoritarian role thrust upon the caseworker by law, must always be based on the fundamental casework principles of mutual respect between client and caseworker, and the responsibility of the caseworker to symbolize the reality of the client to his client.

Chapter Twelve

Supervision

Supervision may be considered a different kind of clinical process with a special focus. The supervisor helps the student or social worker in training to develop and grow.

This implies first an extension of knowledge of human behavior and therapeutic techniques from the academic to the practical. Never let it be overlooked that supervision is a learning experience—learning facts as well as learning about oneself in relation to others. Therapeutic skills must be taught on a demonstrable basis. As interviews with clients are discussed by supervisor and trainee before and after they are held pertinent, therapeutic techniques are reviewed. Thus an abstract theory is translated into practice, and the supervisor's skills are added to and refined. The skills are essentially those elaborated in previous chapters.

The emphasis on insight is focused sharply on the caseworker's awareness of himself but only in relation to his clients. The causes and contributing factors in the worker's personal life are irrelevant to this process. The overflow of these patterns of behavior into the social and familial situation are equally irrelevant. Any observed pattern of behavior, no matter how disturbed, is not within the purlieu of the supervisory process unless it is affecting that particular worker's relationship with his client or clients. It is true that the worker himself often becomes aware of how the emotional reaction and behavior which affects his working with clients positively and adversely is also reflected in his behavior outside the agency. It is then his responsibility to seek therapeutic help for himself if he so desires. Many social workers do. But this decision must remain the privilege of the individual caseworker. The supervisor must only be careful that the supervisory process does not become personal therapy for the supervisee. It is very easy for the inexperienced or nondisciplined supervisor to slip over the fine line that exists between the two. But awareness of the differences will help the supervisor hew closely to his own well-delineated role. The principles of diagnosis, resistance, transference and use of relationship, are all utilized in the service of the development of the worker. The supervisor who has been trained to be sharply, acutely and diagnostically disciplined in his work with clients will have little difficulty in transferring these modes of functioning to the act and practice of supervision.

The supervisor begins with previous evaluations of the worker's strengths and weaknesses. The more sharply focused the selection of the emphasis for supervision of any particular worker, the greater will be the learning and the more effective the supervision. Worker and supervisor can then cooperate in the resolution of a problem that is consciously troubling both.

The protection of the agency's client is the primary responsibility of the supervisor. This is different from and parallel to the personal development of the social work trainee into a disciplined, self-aware professional person. Self-awareness is not of much value unless there is sufficient technical knowledge as well. The schools of social work accept and carry out the task of transmitting this knowledge by translating the theory into practice. Step by step the supervisor follows the beginning worker with an alert and acute eye on the needs of the client. Insofar as possible, the worker in training is assigned clients whose needs can be met by the supervisee's skills. Supervisory conferences prior to the first meeting of worker and client are geared to the mutual recognition of the focus and goals of treatment, as indicated by the intake interview. Emphasis on prompt recording to make the results of an interview immediately available to the supervisor is both protection of the client and the imposition of professional discipline on the worker. As the worker grows, he is given more and more freedom and, hopefully, less and less supervision. Just as the goal for a client, whatever his problem, is independence from the worker, so the goal for the worker is independence from the supervisor.

The basic techniques and skills of social casework that need to be taught have been discussed at length by others in the field of social work education. They do not need repetition here. The special techniques of diagnostically focused casework treatment have been enumerated in previous chapters. It is the special therapeutic process that molds the professional self-awareness of the individual social worker that merits some special attention. As has been repeatedly stated, each of us has his prejudices and his blind spots. It is our moral and ethical responsibility as social workers not to impose these on our clients. We must be equally careful not to impose our personal standards of morality upon them. We assume an awesome responsibility when we venture to accept the dependency that clients necessarily must thrust upon us. It is the supervisor's responsibility to see that this responsibility is carried out with the fullest awareness of each individual's right to self-determination within the limits of reality. It is this last element that can be as easily distorted by the worker as by the client—and with the best intentions. For example, a worker who has deep religious conviction and is working in a church-supported agency must learn that every client has the right to make up his own mind about religion. This is true about divorce, adoption, marriage, educational and vocational choices. The list is endless. But basic to all of these is the worker's respect for his client's right to make a choice. It is the client's reality that each worker must learn to perceive correctly. This must not only be accepted intellectually in principle but must be hammered home time and time again as the supervisor notes the unconscious evasions of that principle. In this way the supervisor is both protecting the client and increasing the professional discipline of the worker.

Probably the most difficult emotion a social worker must learn to tolerate is hostility. Young inexperienced workers are often greatly shaken by the more violent outbursts of their clients. Again they may have thought they accepted the principle that clients must be free to ventilate their feelings. Experiencing the impact of someone else's affect, especially if the worker happens to be included as the target of that affect, is another matter entirely. Here the age old social work question that has been the subject of so much jesting becomes pertinent for the worker. How does he feel about it? He needs the catharsis of ventilation which only his supervisor can provide. Colleagues are often used as immediate recipients of the steam that needs to be blown off right after the interview that has been disturbing to the worker. But it is the special task of the supervisor to help the worker recognize the sources of his own anxiety—again on a conscious level only as it applies to the reality of the social work situation.

Inexperienced workers are also apt to become excessively disturbed by social conditions, including agency procedures, which they feel are detrimental to or disadvantageous to their clients. This kind of identification has to be interpreted in the light of the supervisor's understanding of a particular worker. But every worker has to learn the hard way that the need to separate from his own subjective reactions, his responsibility to his clients to represent reality, no matter how harsh, with understanding and respect for the client to react in his own individually determined emotional pattern. He also must learn his other responsibility as a professional member of society to face the task of working to change what he knows better than many others needs to be changed. Thus he learns to wear two hats—one in his interviews with his clients—the other in his interviews with his community, whether that be a board of directors, his professional associations, or his political leaders, et al. He must learn that confusion of these two roles leads to confusion for his clients.

The following extract from a family agency record illustrates the dual role of the supervisor in protecting the client and helping a worker become aware of himself. While the quotations from the record are exact, the supervisory comments are hypothetical. This is the record of a 15 year old adolescent assigned to an inexperienced worker. The worker had given evidence of being warm, perceptive and a willing and good student. She showed signs of maturity in her relationship with staff and co-workers. The summary quoted below was prepared by the caseworker.

Norma was referred by the juvenile police in May, 1963, after spending a few days in Juvenile Hall. She had been picked up as a run away. This was the climax of the acting-out she had been doing for the past year, which included fighting, truanting, curfew violations, and hanging around with questionable companions. Norma had asked to be put in a foster home, but the police put her on probation and she was to live with her father, who has her legal custody. It was felt that Norma, who has above-average potential, was beset with emotional problems that might be worked through. Counseling was not made a condition of probation but was strongly recommended to both parents and the girl. The parents then came together to request help here for Norma.

At intake both parents indicated their ambivalence about Norma's behavior and their willingness to have the agency supplant them. Both were alcoholics who used Norma for an expression of their individual unconscious needs, the father provoking sexual acting-out, the mother encouraging outbursts of hostility and rebellion. The parents were divorced and Norma had thoroughly learned how to manipulate one against the other to her own discomfort. Why her distressful cry for foster home placement was ignored at intake is unknown. This decision was made by the court. The agency had no jurisdiction in this area. But we must bear in mind that truly adequate foster homes are not readily available.

For four months Norma was seen by another worker. During this period Norma was not very communicative but showed a recognition of her need for help. Except for brief mention of her parents' alcoholism, interviews seem to have focused on Norma's reality problems at school and with friends. Objective discussion was mistaken for warmth and real understanding. No real progress was made. In August she was assigned to the present worker, Miss Alden, towards whom she seems to have responded with much more feeling. An early entry records, "She has been able to express the feeling that no one really knows her or understands her. Furthermore, people seem more concerned about getting her to change and fit into their expectations, rather than finding out what she wants." The worker listened but did not hear. The discussion of "reality" continued.

Norma continued her associations with other rebellious, impulse-acting-out high school students. Her relationships with her parents and stepfather (her mother had recently remarried) were "stormy." At one point, Norma became angry with the worker for seemingly betraying Norma's trust. The worker responded by discontinuing interviews with the father. It would seem that already Miss Alden was beginning to be, in truth, Norma's sole functioning parent. But she was also unconsciously offering herself to Norma for manipulation. This had to be the subject of a supervisory conference.

> Norma telephoned . . . to tell me that she was very angry with me and did not want to return here. She stated that it seems that I told everything she told me to her father when he came. When I wondered what she had reference to, Norma stated that I had told her father about the drinking party and about "everything else."

(It is to be noted that previously Norma had complained that father pressured her to tell him all about the sessions at the agency.)

> I was rather surprised about this, since Mr. B. had been at the drinking party and I could not

see any secrecy in the matter, since Norma had
told me about it herself. I asked Norma to come
in the same afternoon so that we could talk
about what it was that was making her angry.

Norma was quite direct in expressing her
anger and was able to say that she felt betrayed,
when her father represented the two of us as
being in alliance against Norma. I pointed out
the reasonableness of such a condition from my
own behavior.

. . . I pointed out that realistically I had had
nothing to do with her fate, and had no authority over her. She brought up the matter of trust,
which was why she was extremely angry with
me, as she put it. She began by saying that her
friends knew of a girl on probation who had
trusted her probation officer and she was pun-
ished for it eventually. Relating this to herself
with my help, she felt she didn't know if she
could trust me.

The interview was concluded with the worker's agree-
ment to transfer the father to another worker.

In the supervisory hour it became clear that the worker
had herself a deep involvement in being a better parent
to Norma than Norma's parents had been. Assuming a
parental role can be an overwhelming experience for a
young worker. This, then, was selected as the focus for
supervisory sessions. Miss Alden was frightened by
Norma's anger, fearful that the relationship that had
been building up would be destroyed. She therefore had
been somewhat apologetic on the phone to be certain to
get Norma back into the office. Miss Alden granted an
immediate interview because of her own anxiety about
Norma's anger. But it was also true that the immediacy
of the session was important and essential for Norma.
Norma needed to test the worker's readiness to accept her

anger and any delay would have meant rejection. Both negative and positive aspects of this were recognized in the supervisory hour.

Norma was permitted to express her anger, but the supervisor raised some question about the timing of the worker's defense of herself. Again the worker's anxiety was permitted to be expressed. The worker had been unable to recognize the full extent of Norma's testing. Not only was she trying to find out whether the worker would accept her anger, she was also testing how well she, Norma, could use her anger to manipulate the worker as she had done so successfully with her parents. The worker's anxiety betrayed her. Norma was successful. The relationship was more secure but on an unhealthy, emotional basis. With the ventilation and acceptance of her own anxiety, the worker seemed able to learn more about the difficult pseudoparental role a social worker must assume with adolescents. Miss Alden gained in personal security and learned something about adolescent ambivalence and testing of who is in control. Both of these were the foci of lengthy supervisory conferences.

Miss Alden was able gradually to become more firm with Norma. She encouraged Norma to move from her father's sexually oppressive home to the mother's apartment, which Norma would have to share with mother and stepfather. This lesser of two evils seemingly was somewhat less threatening. Norma's attitudes towards her friends began to be more discriminatory, and her grades at school showed improvement. Presumably the worker was quite active in encouraging Norma towards these goals. She was able to be a stronger parent with whom Norma could identify.

In October, Norma used a battle with her stepfather, which had resulted in her glasses being broken, as an excuse to be absent from school. "I got angry with her and said she should not cut classes . . . that her eyes were not so bad by her own admission that she could not do some work." A few days later in the next session it is recorded:

> In the meantime Norma had difficulty with the school authorities. . . . Norma was attempting to lure some children off the school grounds to ditch school.
> This incident provided dramatic proof to Norma of the difficulty she puts herself in with her impulsive acting out. I was able to point out that her adjustment that she is making is ultimately harmful to herself. She did experience a lot of discomfort this past week and was able to see part of this. We talked directly about her own provocative behavior and her own responsibility and the difficulties she finds herself. I pointed out how she annoyed me so much that I had felt like slapping her, and did it verbally. She seemed able to follow along with this.

Again in the following supervisory hour the positives as well as the negatives were discussed. It was important for Norma to gain insight into her self-motivated destructive behavior. But the worker's pride in her honesty with Norma had to be shattered when the supervisor questioned why the worker had felt like slapping Norma. The worker needed time to recognize how intense was her own involvement. Unwittingly she had intensified Norma's gratification in using delinquent behavior to excite a negative response in those towards whom she Norma felt warmth and affection. There was some value to be gained, however, in the worker's admission to Norma of hostile fantasies that did not need to be acted out.

Following this session, Norma became much more communicative about her past history and present feelings. She felt much more sure of her hold on the worker in a healthy as well as a neurotic sense and therefore could be more giving of herself.

During the last recorded fight "Norma called to ask me to do something about her mother, who was 'in a hysterical fit'—screaming and crying. After consulting with Mrs. P. (mother's worker) we decided that intervention with mother possibly drunk might result in antagonism from mother to Norma and perhaps also create guilt in mother, so that she would never come back to the agency. I called Norma back and explained this to her directly; I increased my availability to her by offering to eat dinner with her and to provide space in the agency where she could study if conditions were intolerable at home at the moment. Norma decided that mother and stepfather were sufficiently quieted down and that she could remain. . . .

"This is the first time that Norma was able to stay in the difficult home situation without running away. She does seem to be more comfortable in her work here and is making use of the relationship with me. I have been working with a double focus; on the one hand I have been trying to help Norma understand perhaps what was the meaning of the significant adult, in an effort to help her accept their acting out in a more objective way. On the other hand, I have been working on her own feelings and naming her acting-out directly what it is. I have been trying to help her understand some of the patterns of coping that she has learned in her family. She seems surprised to be confronted with the similarity of her behavior to that of her parents; she was able to see that their way of coping is generally to deny the realities of what is happening and to flee. . . . It caused her some anxiety to be confronted with her own use of herself in a different way, but basically with the same purpose."

In the final supervisory hour to be considered here, the worker was again confronted with her own anxiety and her need to supplant Norma's own parents. Norma was once again testing the worker's willingness to be manipulated into taking sides and succeeding. The intensity and the extent of the worker's response to what she felt Norma was suffering in both these dreadful homes, indicated a greater depth of understanding of herself in relationship to Norma and all other adolescents who had suffered as had the worker. The supervisor agreed that identification with a client made the limits of the professional relationship more difficult. In this way the supervisor without rejection or hostility, directed the discussion away from the worker's personal problems back to the needs of adolescent clients for a parental authority toward whom they cannot act out their neurotic conflicts successfully. Out of this very frustration comes the learning of a new pattern of relating to important adults and people in general. This term *necessary frustration* now became meaningful for this worker and she could spontaneously see that in the summing-up of her focus in the treatment of Norma, she had ignored the anger that Norma needed so badly to ventilate. The "naming" of Norma's behavior—thievery for joyriding—was really anger on the part of the worker that Norma was not a better-behaved daughter. Yet this was accompanied by sufficient warmth and evidence of acceptance that it was not entirely a roadblock to growth and development for Norma. Norma's fear of her own anger and her great need to be loved became clearer. The worker also eventually learned the danger of substituting dependency for compassion and understanding. Norma was able to tolerate her most difficult situation without having dinner with the caseworker. This worker will learn to respect those strengths beforehand instead of following a demonstration of strength by the client. The essential focus for this particular person, namely 15-year-old Norma, had to be respect for her own right to disapprove and resist her parents' methods of dealing with conflict. Out of this understanding of her own fears, hostilities and anxieties, and with the worker's support and understanding of herself (here we refer to both Norma and the caseworker), will come true understanding and tolerance of the parents.

Thus we see the duality of learning technical skills combined with personal insight on a professional basis. Supervisory sessions are as sharply focused as therapeutic sessions. The more concentrated the learning process, the sooner does growth become possible. Both client and supervisor grow in ego strength awareness of reality and the distortions they are utilizing unwittingly. As the supervisee learns about his distortions, he is freer to help dissolve his clients'.

Conclusion

The supervisor, in effect, retraces the steps of the caseworker, but the cast of characters is changed. A client comes or is sent to an agency because he is experiencing some kind of pressure. The worker diagnoses the cause of that pressure in the light of his perception of the client's reality. He helps the client select the area of help in which both will cooperate in order to restore homeostasis or satisfying functioning. Involved in this process are recognition of affect and distortion of which the client had been previously unaware. These are affected by the factors of resistance and transference. Recognition and ventilation lead to a higher level of integration.

The trainee or beginning worker comes to an agency because he wishes to learn how to be more helpful to people. The caseworker in training is experiencing various kinds of pressures due primarily to his incomplete knowledge of himself as well as of his clients. The supervisor diagnoses the primary source of that discomfort and together with the worker selects the area in which both will cooperate in order to improve the functioning and professional qualification of the caseworker. Involved in this process are recognition of professional reality as well as the effect and distortions of which the caseworker had been previously totally or partially unaware. This, too, is affected by the factors of resistance and transference. Catharsis and insights lead to increased professional growth and development.

Chapter Thirteen

Consultation

Consultation comes in many shapes, forms and sizes. The term is used to describe varied casework functions. There is the consultant status, used primarily as a personnel device to designate a somewhat higher level supervisory position. This is differentiated from other consultant positions because it is a position within an agency and frequently implies responsibility for evaluation of staff members. Then there is the specialist consultant who is responsible for a specific body of knowledge regarding a single area of social work function or interest. Thirdly, there is the administrative consultant who is responsible for specific programs in a legal and technical manner.

Here we are concerned with the casework consultant otherwise known as mental health consultant, psychiatric casework consultant or community-oriented consultant. The variety of names reflects the comparative recent origin of the position and the confusion regarding the many-faceted approaches to the consultation process. Actually casework consultation to individuals and groups has been going on for many years, but its use was limited. Now with the widespread use of the consultation process, it is receiving a great deal more attention and attempts are being made to refine and define the process.

Consultation may be given by a professional to non-professionals or by a better-trained and more experienced professional to other caseworkers. What is most important, besides the background and skill of the consultant, is that he *not* be identified with the agency or group with whom he is meeting. It is the very lack of identification that enables the consultant to maintain the same objectivity that is essential to the client-caseworker relationship.

The tendency to separate reality needs from emotional needs, and vice versa, has become less and less tenable. Any service is therapeutic that attempts to help individuals, families, and/or groups to achieve a mode of living with themselves and with others, that is more satisfying to all concerned. The caseworker therefore needs to be aware of the community, its resources, and what social workers can contribute to make these resources more practically meaningful and more available. The caseworker must also be aware of the individual needs, limitations and cultural and personal differences of each of his clients. The consultant needs to know all these, plus how the caseworker's dynamics affect them.

Because of the large numbers of persons needing assistance of some kind, compared to the small number of trained social workers, inservice training programs are often essential and are included as part of job responsibilities. Public tax-supported agencies necessarily involve the largest numbers of persons receiving and administering various kinds of aid. Even in our more "humane" society, tax dollars are spent sparingly for human services, and caseloads are large. Because of this, and the need to fulfill many legally determined requirements, even trained workers necessarily develop a somewhat limited approach to their services. Each agency has limited functions determined by law or by policy, and the caseworker learns to function within these.

The social worker trained in the treatment of emotional disturbances of individuals and with roots in the interaction between society and its citizens, develops an acute awareness of the pressures on both staff and clients. The social worker functioning as mental health consultant is not bound by the pressures of legal requirements or agency policy and can therefore look at every situation presented with far more objectivity. Recommendations take the reality of both client and agency into consideration. The first question is what would be best; second, how do reality and practical considerations make necessary alterations in what would be "ideal."

The reality of client and agency hopefully includes:

1. An understanding of the individual's dynamics which influence his reaction to the troubled situation.

2. An understanding of the social milieu within which this developed.

3. An understanding of the pressures upon agency and worker and the workers' reactions to these. These vary from an overidentification with clients to an overidentification with those elements in our society hostile to recipients of assistance.

4. An understanding of the social pressures within a community that are reflected in agency policy and legislation.

The consultant must assume the responsibility for this broad point of view. The word *understanding* is most important. With an awareness of all these variables, the consultant is in a position to elicit the pertinent details from the agency staff. This, in turn, increases the understanding of the staff and leads to more respectful and efficient functioning.

It is also possible on occasion to learn how to distill broad mental health principles into a form more consistent with the time limitations of the pressured worker, trained or untrained. The need for more skillful diagnostic thinking is apparent in whatever type of agency this social worker has served. This "honing down" of casework skills can be one of the most meaningful contributions the social worker can make as mental health consultant. As the social worker becomes more and more keenly aware of the precise therapeutic focus, he will be able to help more people more quickly.

In a public assistance agency, a worker making a routine check on a family found them greatly disturbed by the father's paranoid episode the night before. The worker immediately began to make plans for the family and handed out a number of referrals to other agencies. These had much logic, but no attempt was made to find out what the family felt and wanted to do about the situation. The worker was primarily aware of the need to hurry and get things done. There did not seem to be enough time to give this family an opportunity to participate in the planning. Staff discussion of the question of time, ventilation of their feelings about being harassed, helped make them aware of their effect upon the harassed family. It was concluded that the time it might take to help a family plan meaningfully for the referral was more than balanced by the time wasted repeating ineffectual referrals.

Often an awareness of mental health principles will not increase the time spent but make the actual moments with the client more meaningful. A mother in a well-baby clinic became angry at being kept waiting. She had a history of postpartum depression. The social worker, trying to be protective, checked on the woman's appointment and reassured her that she was not being overlooked but would be called soon. A few moments later, the woman left and never returned. The history revealed that although she had suffered many deprivations and rejections, this young woman had never been able to let herself become angry. The mental health consultant was able to point out that recognition of the patient's right to be angry and that it was difficult to be kept waiting might have been an important first step in relieving this woman of her guilt about anger. Here we have the principles of awareness and understanding that can be fitted into the existing structure of our public agencies.

Consultation may be to a staff or a single worker. The consultant's primary responsibility is to extend the worker's knowledge about his clients and to help him sharpen his skills in the application of that knowledge. This includes a worker's self-awareness as it pertains to his professional functioning. These basic principles apply to consultations to staffs as well. However, there are differences, just as there are similarities and differences between individual and group therapy. The consultant must aim to know how this particular group of people functions together within the limits set by agency reality. A consultant is chosen because her knowledge and experience are potentially valuable to a staff. It is her responsibility to share this in the role of instructor. Her major responsibility is less to the client than to the staff. The client is, hopefully, helped by the extension of the worker's skills and knowledge that results from the teaching of the consultant. The supervisors of the less mature worker will be responsible for integrating the consultant's teaching into the ongoing practice of these workers. The mature workers will be able to do this for themselves or be aware enough to discuss whatever troubles them with a supervisor or colleague, or to raise questions with the consultant.

The consultant utilizes the case material to illuminate the teaching focus. Just as in work with clients, the preceding experience, here of the staff, is utilized as a foundation upon which is built increased knowledge. A staff may need to explore its feelings about the limits within which it must work before the staff members are emotionally ready to learn more about how they can help their clients within these limits. One important advantage of the consultant in this situation is the same that the worker has in casework with his clients. She is not experiencing the discomfort and conflict of the situation and pressures that produce the problem selected as the focus of discussion.

Like the client, a staff needs to be accepted where it is and hopefully be helped to develop to a higher level of functioning. The consultant can only help a staff if he has a sound basis of knowledge of how this particular group of people functions within the limits set by its reality: agency regulations, and so on. What seems to be most disturbed in the relationship of this staff to its milieu? The setting as well as the service merits careful attention.

The nature of and reasons for the request for consultation, the attitudes of the staff and supervisors towards the limits within which they have to work, the kinds of case records chosen for presentation—all contribute to the consultant's diagnostic evaluation of how and where she can be most helpful to this particular staff. The cooperative process of selection clarifies for both staff and consultant how they will work together. The consultant evaluates the reality of the staff as well as the affects and distortions of which the staff had previously been unaware. Equally, the process of consultation is affected by the factors of resistance and transference. Catharsis and insight are of prime importance in the growth and development of a staff.

In consultation with the social work staff of a mental hospital, many aspects of work with varying types of psychotics were discussed case by case at regular meetings with the consultant. The primary and essential focus was the realistic institutional problem of interdisciplinary relationships. The workers were free to ventilate their feelings about their frustrations and were encouraged to explore ways in which, within the limits of these frustrations, they could structure situations more helpful to their clients and more satisfying to themselves. Out of these discussions emerged a feeling of mutual respect that made teaching easier, and eliminated, to a large extent, some of the resistances to learning. The ways in which knowledge and self-awareness of staff members, trained and untrained, can be extended may seem numerous. But these can be reduced to a basic principle of adapting the skills of the practitioners to the needs of the people whom they serve.

A public health social worker had established a good relationship with Mrs. Y., a 24-year-old mother of four small children. She had been deserted by her husband but was still dominated by her mother-in-law who lived next door and who interfered constantly in the rearing of the children. Mrs. Y. had begun to use the children as literal whipping boys as an outlet for her mounting frustrations. There was considerable concern about the safety of the children, as well as indications that Mrs. Y. might be heading for a serious depression. The public health nurse, who was also involved in the situation, attended the conference. Mrs. Y. was receiving public assistance. The possibility of encouraging her to move was discussed and discarded for practical reasons. The roles of mothers and mothers-in-law in the Spanish-American culture were discussed, and it became evident that Mrs. Y. could use the support of the social worker in emancipating herself. She was bright, had shown interest in new training programs, and had evidenced use of the relationship with the social worker as a means of establishing a new identity for herself. The manner in which the social worker used herself as a resource consultant for Mrs. Y. was supportive and permissive, even though their sessions together were only biweekly. At the same time, specific instructions were suggested to the public health nurse, which, transmitted to Mrs. Y., helped reinforce her efforts to be a parent. The ways in which the mother could avoid permitting the children to provoke her into a struggle for power with them and with the grandmother were rehearsed together. They were reminded that all children need to test their strength in this regard at times, and that Mrs. Y. would need much support from all concerned in learning to resist provocation and to trust her own strength. In actuality the nurse and social worker would become benign parent surrogates temporarily until Mrs. Y. had the strength to manage her situation alone. A follow-up two months later indicated this plan was working well.

In another instance a group of nurses was bewildered because a patient with a positive Pap smear refused referral to a surgical clinic. They were naturally concerned that if the patient delayed too long, the malignancy might spread. A review of the history indicated that a grandparent had died a lingering painful death after radical surgery for cancer. With this recognition, the nurses were able to see for themselves the necessity of discussing this patient's fears as natural to her and then educating her regarding the differences between her situation and that of her grandfather. Their own anxieties, as opposed to the patient's, became clearer.

The emphasis on cultural differences is an important and constant contribution of the mental health consultant. These, in essence, are no more or less important than any past experience of the client that is pertinent to the presenting problems and modes of resolution. In one community, a social worker was experiencing repeated hostility from unwed mothers, which she was unable to understand. Discussion revealed that these young women came from a small subculture where marriage was rare and men were generally unimportant in the social scheme. Because these were Caucasians, not usually identified with a matriarchal culture, the worker was not aware that her question regarding possible placement of the unborn baby immediately made her a representative of a "foreign"—hostile—point of view.

In another matriarchal cultural group, a mother and her four daughters lived together. All four daughters had children but no husbands. All received public assistance. The youngest, aged 20, with two children, wanted to break away. The public health social worker was able to intercede with the public assistance agency to secure a separate rental allowance for her. She was also able to make available to Miss V. knowledge of resources for job training and of housekeeping services to make the job training possible. The worker was anxious about her inability to give Miss V. sufficient time to ventilate her guilt and hostility about being the first to break away from the traditional pattern. With the support of the consultant, the worker could accept that the acknowledgment of these feelings in the limited time spent with Miss V. plus her obvious activity in behalf of and at the behest of the client were serving much the same purpose. Often nonverbal activity has as much value as verbal.

The social worker who has herself refined her skills as a practitioner can teach these refinements in varied settings. The "social" aspects of the caseworker's training are invaluable assets for the mental health consultant. The extensions of the aforementioned principles to administrative and community consultation have necessarily been omitted due to limitations of space. These deserve a chapter all their own.

Because consultation is a burgeoning specialty, it is still in great part a creative process. Some valuable research is being conducted which bears out the value of certain specific types of consultation. Foremost, of course, is Dr. Gerald Caplan's "theme interference" procedure.* Here again diagnosis of the problem is one of the most important tools. But other methods of consultation are being used and found extremely helpful.

1. Patient-oriented consultation where a case is discussed with the consultee solely to extend knowledge of personality dynamics and how this knowledge can be utilized in the setting of the consultee.

2. Patient-oriented consultation with the focus on staff feelings about a problem.

3. Staff-focused consultation aimed at work-attitudinal changes, greater work satisfaction. The focus may be prejudices, personnel fears or similar questions. Reassurance is gained from ventilation and understanding acceptance. This leads to greater awareness and respect for individual differences and again becomes a

*Caplan, Gerald *Approach to Community Mental Health*, New York, Grune & Stratton, 1961.

learning situation with personal growth. Personal growth must always be confined to the requirements of the job.

4. Staff-focused consultation aimed at intrastaff problems. Here the consultant must be extremely cautious to see that personal problems do not spill over into work problems. Again, clear diagnostic thinking is the most helpful safeguard. As consultation proceeds, a greater degree of cooperation amongst members of the group becomes evident. This, then, is the goal and the focus.

5. The consultant serves as a catalyst for the sharing of ideas, feelings and insights on problems of clients and/or staff. The very presence of a benign professional outsider frequently provokes freer discussion and hence informed communication.

The list could almost be as long as the list of consultants and their consultees. What is more important is that the type of consultation be suited to the needs of the consultee, expressed or unexpressed.

For this reason it is important to emphasize that primary to good consultation practice is understanding of the agency or group function by whom consultation is requested. Corollary to his is the important question of who requested the consultation for whom. If, for example, the administration requested consultation for a staff without the latter's knowledge, the consultant must be prepared to face and hopefully overcome a great deal of initial resistance, before real work can begin. Thus along with diagnoses of the request the consultant must aim for clarification of his role. Above all, he must beware of the need of staff to thrust upon him, usually in a hostile manner, the role of omnipotent and omniscient mentor.

Conclusion

An agency requests the services of a consultant because it is uncomfortable with certain aspects of its functioning. This is usually subsumed under the heading of extension of knowledge. This is true. But a good consultant also needs to be aware of other factors. The nature of and reasons for the request, the attitudes of the staff and supervisors towards the limits within which they have to work, the kinds of case records chosen for presentation all contribute to the consultants' diagnostic evaluation of how and where he can be most helpful to this particular staff. The mutual selection clarifies for both staff and consultant how they will work together. The consultant, too, evaluates the reality of the staff as well as the effects and distortions of which the staff had previously been unaware. The process of consultation is equally affected by the factors of resistance and transference. Catharsis and insight are of prime importance in the growth and development of a staff.

Chapter Fourteen

Conclusions

While each modality—individual, family and group therapies; supervision and consultation—has essential differences, there is a consistent thread of similarity in all these varying casework functions. Diagnosis, decision regarding focus, gathering of material for understanding the how and why of the presenting problem, clarification of the caseworker's role, evaluation of distortions, acceptance of the client where he is, are all part of every casework relationship. On the part of the client, supervisee or consultant, ventilation, catharsis, resistance, greater insight, reordering of reality awareness, integration of insights, are all important for his growth and development.

Thus whether the process be therapy, supervision or consultation, the basic processes are only different in application. Faced with a prospective client, supervisee or consultee, the caseworker must first get a history. What is the problem presented? When did it start? What appears to be the real problem as manifested by the symptomatology? Here the focus begins to emerge. As the caseworker discusses this with client, group, supervisee or consultee, the mutual tasks of both become more and more apparent. Here the basic casework principle of "accept the client where he is" becomes operative. Here the decision is made by both parties, as to where the client will go. For purposes of this chapter, hereafter the term client will include all four types of "clients" i.e., individual, group, supervisee or consultee.

The second principle is to learn about the living situation of the client, where and with whom he lives and or works, and how the presenting symptoms affect and in turn are affected by the presenting symptomatology. Clarification of the role of the caseworker includes evaluation of the client's motivation with its correlative negative of resistance to insight and learning. Again the manifestations of these are different, but the basic process remains the same. Ventilation, clarification of distortion, education, support and reassurance are the tools used to promote a more satisfying level of functioning, whether it be on a personal or staff level.

In all of these situations the caseworker must guard against the omnipotent use of the authoritarian role, and the use of jargon as a status symbol. The caseworker is constantly aware of his use of the relationship for or against identification of the client with himself. He sorts out distortions, keeps his interpretations reality-oriented. It is his very objectivity, plus his understanding of the reality as well as of the reasons for the client's distortions, that is so eminently helpful to the client in his search for clarification and greater strength to meet his everyday problems.

As is customary in individual casework therapy, it is also a truism for group, family, supervisory and consultation relationships, that the first interpretations are almost always positive and ego-supporting. This in turn augments the relationship and makes the next less positive interpretations more acceptable. Universality and generalization of problems are techniques that are reassuring and insight-producing to all the groups mentioned.

Finally, the goals of all learning are new insight, knowledge and experience. New ways of reaching solutions are learned. Increased ego strengths gained from these experiences, serve as a firm foundation for more effective and therefore more satisfying functioning.

Thus we isolate the main themes of casework therapy and see their application to supervision and consultation. Caution must be taken that the supervisor and consultation processes do not deteriorate into personal therapy. The material is very different. It is only the basic process that remains the same. The emphasis in therapy is on personal material. Insofar as it is possible, personal material is excluded from supervision and consultation. In supervision it is sometimes admissable when it is work-related. In consultation the emphasis is far more strongly placed on job function to the almost total exclusion of personal material.

A careful examination of many of the so-called new techniques will reveal that they are new only in the sense that the semantics are different. They are variations of well established methods formalized into firm panacea and dressed up in new language. A careful examination of the valuable "new" therapies will reveal that they are elaborations of old techniques already used in the psychotherapy of clinical social work. It is the rigidity of their claims that make them dangerous. Basically, there is value in a rehearsal of old techniques. The new language frequently represents clearer formulations and as such can be very helpful and can be used to make social workers more aware of what they are doing, thus helping to sharpen their skills. They only become harmful when they are used indiscriminately. It is vitally important that the technique be used that is suited to the patient. Hopefully, the client will never be straitjacketed to conform to a technique.

For example, parents who are having problems rearing their children may need educational counseling rather than insightful therapy. A 19-year-old mother with two children was referred to a clinical social worker when her young infant had to be hospitalized for malnutrition. An exploratory intake revealed that she had been reared in a wealthy family in another country. She had had no experience in housekeeping or child rearing but was eager to learn. Her husband had assumed these duties until his desertion a short time before the referral. This young woman spoke little English and did not know how to manage. She had almost exhausted her savings. A homemaker was found to teach this young woman the rudiments of child care and housekeeping. Within six months she was functioning well. The diagnostic clue was, of course, her eagerness to learn. However, a parent who is unable to cope with the responsibilities of childrearing usually needs exploration of the reasons for this, with therapeutic emotional experiences.

A 21-year-old girl who had been completely infantilized by her mother was referred to a clinical social worker after five years of unsuccessful insight therapy. A diagnostic evaluation revealed that her major problem was a lack of self-discipline due to constant and consistent overindulgence by her mother. The caseworker and client then made a list of priorities that had to be learned: (1) no physical acting out of hostility to mother; (2) attendance at classes; (3) competition of school assignments without mother's help; (4) giving up dependence on mother for assistance with various tasks one by

one. Each week, the client would report progress and
failure and receive approval and disapproval. The therapist's approval became important because the client recognized that for the first time a therapist really understood her problem.

The emphasis on the interaction between the client
and important persons in his life is only another way of
telling a client how his behavior is causing problems for
him. The man who is so involved in a love-hate relationship with his deceased father turns all relationships into
a struggle for power. He is so busy proving his superiority that there is no energy left over for forming meaningful relationships, and he complains of loneliness. Constant and persistent interpretations of this whenever his
productions are relevant, produces awareness and
change, but only after emotionally reexperiencing his
ambivalent feelings for his father.

Even the heavily disputed technique of touching can
be valuable at times. The social worker must be ab-
solutely certain that what he is doing will not be considered seductive but will be of benefit to the client and
is relevant to the primary focus of the task to be accomplished. An extremely ugly client who had had a
great deal of plastic surgery was finally convinced that
he was liked by his therapist when the latter once casual-
ly put his arm around him. His need for physical reassurance was clear to the therapist from conscious productions and dreams.

There are times when emphasis on the present is more
important than examination of the past. This is usually
the case where the problem has rather superficial origins
and the pattern to be changed is of comparatively recent
history. The anamnestic exploration will usually reveal
a strong ego which has functioned well until a seemingly overwhelming crisis developed. A man who had been

employed by the same firm for thirty years, lost his job and was widowed all in the same week. The firm went out of business and his wife was killed in an auto accident. He was severely depressed. A referral to a physician for medication and supportive emphasis on the plans that needed to be made to reestablish a new life for himself were all that were needed to help this man. Another individual who might have been overly dependent would certainly need a very different mode of therapy.

The list of "new" therapies is almost endless. We are beset with new ideas almost weekly. This kind of ferment is healthy. It helps us think through what we are doing and why. The more skilled the caseworker, the greater will be her or his ability to analyze the "new" therapies and compare them with the "old." And the greater will be his skill in adopting what is useful and discarding what is gimmickry. An important slogan should be: Fit the technique to the patient; never try to mold the patient's needs to fit any technique.

The next great innovative contributor to psychotherapy after Freud will be the still-unknown hero who will devise a research model that will truly correlate treatment and symptoms with a guide to sorting out the multiplicity of factors present in each individual's personality. Until such time, we must hear each individual with respect for his uniqueness, sharpen our diagnostic thinking and be alert to the need to correlate or change our hypotheses as the client's productions unfold.

Perhaps the key word is pertinence. In every setting, casework service is geared to what is pertinent to the presenting problem and to what is mutually decided upon as a desirable goal. The more sharply focused the therapy, supervision or consultation, the greater will be the economy of joint effort and the more effective will be the results.

Index

213